Welcome to the

State of Kuwait

Francesca Spencer

For teachers everywhere.

Contents

Dunning Kruger Syndrome – the selfbelief that you are really brilliant, even though you are actually not.

Preface

"Someone needs to write this stuff down," I remember saying to my flatmate, Tessa. "It's unbelievable."

I was in Kuwait on my first teaching job out of uni, learning very quickly, about all the things they don't teach you in class.

"You do it," said Tessa.

"I am not a writer."

Unconsciously, I started to collect stories from my own experiences and to steal them from people around me. These anecdotes form the outline loosely following the timeframe of a school year - September to June. It appears to be one year, although my contract was two, and I have arranged the stories and events to fit.

The characters, observations and happenings are all real. I have done my best to be truthful and authentic with my storytelling, but for the purposes of a good read, I have tweaked here and there, embellished and added detail of my own imaginings, as you do.

Welcome to the State of Kuwait offers an insight of a culture and country at odds with itself. The meaning of 'state' in the title refers to the 'condition of', as in *the state of the teenager's bedroom*, rather than the political organisation of the country. In effect, the book is about three states: the state of my personal microcosm, the state of the world of the school where I taught and the state of the country itself, forming the backdrop to it all.

The headings for each chapter deal with a particular aspect of life in Kuwait and I have indulged myself with hefty dollops of comment and opinion. Why not? It's my book.

It is not meant to be, in any way, a sociological or academic text. I wrote it to see if I could, but mostly as entertainment for anyone who wants to know what it is really like teaching on the international circuit, with Kuwait as an example.

I could not have completed this book without a whole heap of wonderful people.

Firstly, I have to thank my family who put up with me, gave me a bed and access to a well-stocked fridge. I am forever indebted to your collective kindness. I have to thank the amazing people I talked and laughed with during my time in Kuwait. Thank you for sharing your stories; I hope I have done them justice. A big thank you goes to Richard for proof reading. Thanks heaps, to the very talented Melanie who agreed to design the cover. Thank you to my friends who encouraged my efforts. And a final thank you to mum, whose enthusiasm for this project was borderline nagging.

I am not a writer. But someone had to write it all down. So here it is.

I hope you enjoy it, and if you do, please pass it on.

(Names have been changed to protect...me.)

1

Arrival

Fuck… Off.

Aaaallllaaaaaaaaahhhhhhu akkbah!!!

There it was again. The over-amplified call to prayer jolts me awake. I reach for my phone. It's four in the morning. I close my eyes and try to get back to sleep. It's my first day in Kuwait.

Anyone who says they are here for any other reason than to make some cash is lying. There is literally no other reason to be here. For teachers, the pull to the Middle East is highly attractive as the packages on offer are potentially lucrative. The recruitment companies advertise with wow words that work - *tax-free, accommodation and utilities provided, annual return flights, full medical insurance*. It's hard not to be seduced by this sweet deal and for me, homeless and penniless; a job in one of the oil-rich nations was a no-brainer.

In addition to these obvious financial benefits, the humble classroom teacher has a wonderfully fluid timetable and only has to plan, teach and assess four subjects; English, Maths, Science and either History or Geography, depending on the term. The other subjects – Art, P.E., I.C.T., Music - are nicely farmed out to the specialist teachers. Compared to the workload of my peers in New Zealand, who are obliged to teach all subjects and can only stay on top of things if they take work home; are in school most weekends; are expected to run after-school activities and go on camp - my timetable is a breeze.

The school calendar is also quite appealing for a slacker like me who enjoys as much time off as I can get away with. At one hundred and seventy eight days of contact time, the school year is really little more than half a year.

Hooray! I'm in. Where do I sign?

I didn't know much about Kuwait before coming here, other than it is very small: with a population of around four million it is barely more than a big town on the coast, bordered by Iraq and Saudi Arabia and across a thin stretch of the Arabian Gulf from Iran. It was a low key sort of place with nothing much apart from sand and oil when suddenly in 1990 this tiny place became focus of the world's attention as Saddam Hussein invaded, igniting the first of the Gulf Wars. Since liberation, a year later, Kuwait returned to being its tiny self and off the media radar.

I looked for information online and found not very much. On a casual browse, Kuwait was described by some travel websites as 'authentically Arab' and an 'intriguing destination' with a rich history in the 'cradle of civilization', but overall the message about Kuwait was ho-hum for the potential visitor/ tourist. Still, being naturally nosy, I was excited to go and find out for myself about the real Kuwait.

Having accepted a post, I still didn't have much idea of what to expect from the country, or the school. I had done a Google search, of course, and found the only comments about the school were negative. 'If they offer you a contract, DO NOT ACCEPT!', 'you have been warned!' being my favourites. I optimistically reasoned that a minority of people who have had a bad experience are more likely to post a comment than the majority of people that have had a good experience. I took this feedback with a hearty pinch of salt and boarded a flight to begin my first teaching job out of university, in the Great Unknown – Mangaf, Kuwait City.

Mangaf is the second-to-last suburb south before the oil refinery which marks the city limits. It is a good forty-five minutes taxi ride from the airport and judging by the size and quality of dwellings, is one of the less desirable areas. It's a ghetto of dusty, low-cost apartments, built to accommodate the immigrant population of boiler-suited shift workers who daily bus in and out of the refinery and related industry.

I am dropped off at my new home and handed a key.

The school-provided accommodation is very comfortable and feels like a mid-range holiday apartment. For me, this is luxury, considering I have just spent six months on a camp bed in the lounge at my family's home in London. While there, I accumulated some classroom experience as a supply teacher as I searched for an international posting. I didn't have to wait long before I was offered a job in Kuwait that filled all my requirements: lush accommodation being high on my wish list.

The spacious, light, airy eighth floor pad is close to heaven. It is fully furnished with new beds and bedroom furniture, washing machine, fridge, microwave, a dining suite, coffee table, and TV, all still in plastic wrapping. There are two sofas which unfortunately are not new, but I am big enough to overlook this minor flaw because this beautiful flat comes rent-free. I can't help smiling when I say the words aloud. And also, I can't really complain considering how much I would be spending for a similar place in London or even New Zealand. It is clear that there is no way I would be able to afford such lavish living on a newly qualified teacher's salary, anywhere in the rent-paying western world. However, this is a two bedroom flat, so at some point I will have to share, but right now I have the place all to myself.

Outside the lounge window is the mosque, which occupies an otherwise empty piece of land. It's not so much a designated open public area, such as a park or a sports ground, it's more a yet-to-be-built-on lot used mostly as a car park and rubbish dump. The implications of having a mosque so close did not hit home until the early hours of that first morning when the muezzin's amplified call to prayer seemed to be right next to my head and turned up to eleven. Since that first early morning awakening, I learned to go to bed wearing earplugs, but over time I became accustomed to the racket of our noisy neighbours and could sleep right through the distorted wailings.

The vacancy of the yet-to-be-built-on desolate land affords the *Ivory Tower* (what the flat became known as) wonderful views of clear blue skies fading to rust-orange sunsets against a skyline of apartment blocks, telecommunication towers, pylons, satellite dishes, water tanks and cranes. Tail lights of traffic queues, scrubby trees, dusty palms, and further in the distance, the yellow ever-burning gas torches of the refinery, splash colour in an otherwise backdrop of beige.

It occurs to me that I don't know my address. Apart from the major roadways, there are no street names in the less salubrious residential suburbs of Kuwait. As in some futuristic novel, residential areas are organised in apartment blocks, which are numbered, on streets which are numbered, in suburbs, which are named and divided into areas or blocks, which are numbered. For example, Flat 25, building 16, Salwa, Block 2. This is a system that would seem to work, but I have noticed, in my immediate neighbourhood, there are two Street 22s.

Before I figure out the building/ street/ block/ suburb pattern, I live at *Dead Cat Corner* because of a ginger cat that was freshly killed soon after my arrival. The furry corpse laid out where it had died would visually mark the passage of time: its eyes disappearing first and its mouth pulled back into a savage, macabre smile; its body flattened out in mummification and eventual dismemberment, where all that would be left is a windblown tuft of ginger fur caught on a sharp stone.

There is no postal system which really upsets my mum.

"Where do I send your Christmas present?" she asks on the phone in her worried voice.

She wasn't happy about me working in the Middle East. This area of the world is never featured on any 'best place to live in the world' list, but as we know, in western media, the 'news' is always presented heavily pro-western. I acknowledge the stories of ISIS, crimes against humanity and social unrest, but don't give them any more weight than the violent crimes reported from other countries. I refuse to live in fear and besides, an address in Kuwait is statistically a safer option than one in London, a city that has proved on more than one occasion to be a target for terrorism, violence and riot.

Rupert and Sandra are my neighbours across the hall from the Ivory Tower. They arrived on the same flight as me from the U.K. I remember seeing Sandra at Abu Dhabi airport as we waited for a connection, and wondered if she was a teacher, like me. She isn't but her husband, Rupert, who has a shaved head and tattooed arms, turned out to be head of primary, my boss.

Like me, they had been delighted to find that all the furnishings in their apartment were new, excluding the matching sofas, which were faded ochre velour and vintage, but not in a good way. Although they were pretty happy with their new home, their sense of nosiness had got the better of them one evening and, like a couple of mischievous teenagers, they went exploring to see how their flat compared to others in our building. They found that the doors to the as yet unoccupied flats were unlocked, so they seized an opportunity to look round.

In the flat next door, the layout was pretty similar. Things were new in the kitchen, and the beds and bedroom furniture were the same as the ones they had just unwrapped in their own flat. The spaces quietly awaiting the new tenants to put on duvet covers and create a home. The main difference was that the lounge furniture in the next door flat was new and stylish in its clean-lined Swedish design, and still showed off the shop-tag from an arm of each couch.

"We just swapped them over," said Sandra. "Who's going to know?"

The next member of the crew to arrive is Tessa, a smiley twenty-something from Ireland. Tessa and I were instant best friends and discovered we have much in common. We are both travellers, vegetarians and our reason for accepting a teaching job in Kuwait had more to do with its saving potential than a burning desire to educate the Middle East.

Had we succumbed to the dark lure of the tax-free dinar? Had we allowed it to skew our authenticity and warp our motives with its promise of wealth and prosperity? Perhaps. Would this twisted motivation of 'eye on the prize' affect our teaching ability and professional standards? Probably not.

Tessa unpacks and makes herself comfortable in the apartment next door.

That afternoon the doorbell rang. I was scrubbing the kitchen cupboards and had been at it for around five hours. My first impression of spotless modernity in my flat had vanished when I spent some time unpacking the care package that was left for me of cornflakes, bread, milk and butter. I opened one of the cupboards and started to put away the new IKEA cutlery and table ware, when I noticed the streaks of grey grime that I thought, in my bleary jet-lagged state, was just the pattern of the kitchen surface. On closer inspection this brand new apartment building had been fitted with a very used second hand kitchen. It was caked in grease, dust and some sort of gloopy orange matter I could only assume was soup that had been splashed around. It had formed hard crusty globs on the underside of the upper cupboards, which I had done my best to chip off with a knife. I had soaped down and rinsed every surface three times and still grey smears dribbled down. I was close to tears.

"Just a minute!" I yelled, when I heard the happy sound of the doorbell and the welcome possibility of release from my cleaning hell.

I peel off the rubber gloves and, wet with sweat I check the peephole before opening the door.

It was the neighbours.

"We were thinking of going out to find the beach," said Sandra. "It looks like it's only a couple of k from here. You want to come?"

I was red in the face. Sweat was streaming from my head in rivers, running down my neck before sticking my t-shirt to my back. Although there was air-con in the lounge and bedrooms, the kitchen and the bathroom didn't seem to be connected to the cooling system.

"Give me five minutes!" I gushed, grateful.

The four of us gathered in the lobby. Rupert had a print out from Google maps.

"Ok then, we are here, and it looks like the beach is here," he said pointing to lines on the paper.

We set off.

Outside on the street, the heat is heavy and still. Even though it is now dark, the temperature makes a mockery of my shower and I start to sweat immediately.

We walk down the road to the left of our building and come across another mosque and a two-lane highway. Cars speed past, but we all cross safely and continue down a residential street which ends in a dusty vacant lot similar to our own.

There seems to be a repeating pattern or recurring theme of town planning. The mosque is placed in a central block surrounded by a road and apartment buildings. There are one or two *bakala* or convenience stores. There is at least one laundry and a couple of basic Indian restaurants. There are gyms, hair salons and massage parlours for men – *Next Step, Homme, Swiss Gym* - and hair and nail salons for women - *Glam and Glitter, Hollywood Nails* and *Femme Fatale* - on upper floors.

One thing becomes clear. The people who live around here are mostly men, or the men are mostly out and the women are not. I am aware we are being stared at, so I look at the ground. I also look at the ground because there are so many hazards to avoid. Parked cars block the way, broken paving and piles of rubbish create an obstacle course to test balance and agility. There are few footpaths and many holes.

A large, fancy, white late-model car pulls up outside what looks like a hardware store and toots its horn. Household items – metal pots, plastic containers, jugs, cooking utensils, baskets, sleeves of kitchen sponges, mops and brushes adorn the exterior like an installation at the Tate Modern. The driver of the car lowers his window and shouts something into the shop. A man appears in the doorway, someone I assume who works there, and listens to the urgent request of the man in the car. He then disappears into the shop, soon to return with whatever had been requested; perhaps a red plastic bucket.

We get to the end of the street. There is a moment of doubt as Rupert checks our bearings on the map. We look around in all directions like a family of meerkats.

"This way," we agree and scramble over a mound of sand and rubble through a gap in a hedge, cross a six lane highway to a set of lights and there it is - the beach.

Al Kout beach is a public area of sand and palm tree-lined promenade. It is teeming with families sharing picnics, kids with bikes and skates, young men playing volleyball and basketball under streetlights and Arabic men wearing traditional white *dishdasha*, talking on cell-phones. There is a soft onshore breeze which brings vague wafts of a sewer, mingled with gas from the refinery, over the lapping waves. Men and children splash around in the shallows, while Arabic women in black *abaya* or Indian women wearing *sari* sit and watch from the shelved beach.

I kick off my sandals and get my feet wet. The sea is bath-water tepid, an ideal temperature for bacterial growth. I take my chances, enjoying the feeling of sand and sea while keeping a watchful eye for numerous bits of broken glass half buried in the sand.

The walk to Al Kout beach would prove to be a life saver during the year. Knowing I could get my feet wet in the sea, a short walk away from my front door became one of the small pleasures which kept me going in this place of daily challenges.

Over the next few days there were more arrivals to fill up the top floors of our apartment building. P.E. Dave moved into the flat between Tessa's and Rupert and Sandra. He was clearly an alpha male, mid twenties, lots of muscles with a thick Sunderland accent that I had to tune into to understand; most of the time I just nodded and smiled.

"I don't think much of this lounge suite," he said as he dumped his bag looking at Rupert and Sandra's tired, old lumpy discarded sofas.

"Well, you can probably swap with one of the downstairs flats, before the rest of the teachers arrive," said Sandra helpfully.

"C'mon, let's do this thing!" roared Dave and within minutes we were all involved in a mad furniture swap. Old sofas were shifted out of Dave's flat, and brand new sofas from the flat below were moved in. Ordinarily I don't do heavy lifting and I don't quite know why I felt compelled to join in. It must have been the P.E. teacher's bellow that motivated everyone into action and made furniture-moving a team bonding exercise. He convinced us that if we all helped out, we could accomplish the task in the blink of an eye and be settled on new comfy sofas for a cup of tea, a chocolate Hobnob (he had brought a packet from home) and an episode of *Game of Thrones*.

Downstairs on the next floor there was Tim, most definitely not an alpha male, from the Midlands. He was twenty-one, not a qualified teacher and this was his first job out of polytech. He had the look of a frightened rabbit and he found it necessary to repeat everything he said three or four times. Dave, being large of heart as well as body, went out of his way to take Tim 'under his wing' and put up with him long after the rest of us had lost patience. Tim followed Dave around like a loyal dog and Dave, feeling a little bit sorry for Tim, allowed him to hang around, even though he was quietly being driven mad. This pent-up frustration exploded one day when Dave's fist hit the side of the kitchen kettle. The kettle, which Dave assured us was faulty anyway, was placed back in its box and swapped with one from a still-vacant apartment downstairs.

There is a common misconception that someone who is lacking in physically appealing attributes makes up for this deficit by being a 'nice' person or having a 'nice' personality. Tim disproved this theory a number of times. We were all heartily sick of his whining weirdness. For me, avoiding him was easy because his class was far away from mine. Not so for Tessa, who was in the same year group, so she had to endure his presence at least once a week at the year meetings. But, as it turned out, he wouldn't last the distance and left before the year was up.

Dave's flat mate Simon was the next to arrive. He was from Liverpool and informed everyone he met that he had come to Kuwait from Qatar, where he had a very well-paying job teaching secondary science, but the school would not meet his requirements of a multiple exit visa, so he was forced to leave and take this job, even though it didn't pay as much, although he was head of science here, but it was alright under the circumstances, until he could get something else. He was in a position of accepting the first offer that came up, so here he

12

was. Over the next few weeks he would draw whoever was around into his dilemma of whether to stay or go.

He was like an over-sized child, with a frowning resting face and a mouth that was a perfect up-side-down, drawn-on smile.

"I just don't know now," Simon would start, and I knew exactly how the conversation was going to go. I looked around for the nearest exit. "I could stay," he would say raising one hand, palm facing up. "Or, I could go," raising the other hand, palm up, as he, tilting his head from left to right, alternately raising and lowering each hand, giving the impression of a life-sized marionette waiting for divine intervention from the gods of international science teachers.

So here we were, the first to arrive, the core crew of our apartment building about to start a new phase in our lives far from anything normal or familiar. There was an element of being accidently thrown together as in some reality television show where we could be voted off by the audience; or a thriller where random characters are played against each other for the amusement or revenge of an unseen psychopath. Who will survive to the end? Who will die? Who will quit? Who will give a lame medical excuse? Who will go a little bit loopy? Who will watch TV and eat crap? Who will get fat and depressed? Tune in next week to find out.

2

School

The walk to school is not far, but in the baking sun it seems like miles. Even with sunglasses shading my eyes, the light is over-bright and at 6.30am, it is an oven-hot morning. The heat hits as soon as I leave the air-conditioned cool of the apartment building foyer and begin to pick my way along a dusty road with no footpath. At every step, the heat sucks moisture from my skin like salt on a slug. I say a quick hello to the cat corpse which grins back from its stiff flattened state in the dust. I pass stinky skips, holding my breath until I judge I'm a safe distance away on the other side before I dare to breathe normally. I pass a mechanics, an Indian restaurant, a bakala, more apartment buildings, what looks like an air-conditioner repair shop, another Indian restaurant, a barbers, another apartment building, another bakala, a laundry and an arrangement of lounge furniture set out for entertaining at the side of the road. I cross a road past another cat corpse, through a car park beside an Arabic school, through what seems like a strip of desert where there is a low, derelict mud brick house covered in spray-can graffiti, some more high-rise apartments, through another car park and there's the school.

The actual name of the school is inconsequential, and for obvious personal safety and legal reasons I am not going to name it. So here I will ask for some co-operation and a little imagination. Firstly, think of a British long-standing educational institution; an establishment which conjures solid and extremely high academic achievement; a seat of learning steeped in history and grandeur. It doesn't matter what comes to mind, just think of a name. Then put that name in front of *English School*, and tadaaaaah - that is the name of the school! There are many schools in Kuwait that follow this naming formula: choosing a name which is synonymous with academic excellence, to add weight and credibility; to impress prospective parents and therefore fill their classrooms and their bank accounts. The name of the school is as fictional as *Tom Brown's School Days* and has absolutely no real connection to any British place of learning: it is just a name. I will refer to the school as *the school*.

I am one of ten new teachers who have arrived to start work during the past few days. We congregate in the reception area and then are ushered through a corridor, where Arabic people are milling about with their children, buying uniforms and filling in forms. As we pass, someone says, "They must be the new teachers. I hope they stay."

We walk through an open area tiled in beige, which feels like a prison exercise yard, viewed by upper-storey windows on all sides. It is covered by a tent-like shade cloth, which partially blocks out the sun but not the heat. This, we learn, is the quad, the space used for morning assembly, known as flag ceremony, playtime, P.E. and lunch. High up on the walls there are giant photos of Big Ben, a number 52

15

London bus to Willesden Green, a horse guard on parade and a view of the Thames featuring the London eye. As well as the iconic images of London, there are two larger than life-sized photos of the Amir of Kuwait, His Highness Sheikh Sabah Al-Ahmad Al-Jaber Al-Sabah and His Highness Crown Prince Sheikh Nawaf Al-Ahmad Al-Jaber Al-Sabah. They smile down and wave, like a comedy duo, in an attitude of jolly benevolence.

Apart from the quad being like a prison exercise yard, the school building in general has a prison-like or fortress feel to it: mock battlements crown the roof, tiny windows peer out from the walls and a wrought iron gate at the main entrance seems, not to keep people out, but to lock them in. Overall, I can't think of a more hostile or unfriendly environment and I never lost that feeling of doom whenever entered the gates, climbed the steps and walked through the front door.

Up some stairs, we turn right along a corridor, then left and into a small, square room where the only natural light comes filtered, through a window from the corridor, which has a window overlooking the quad. All areas are tiled to waist height in shades of forget-me-not blue, which amplifies any sound and brings to mind hard hitting documentaries investigating orphanages or psychiatric wards.

In the room where we are ushered, there is some dark, anarchic graffiti on two of the walls, depicting what looks like a demon with horns, fiery red eyes and zigzag jagged teeth. We are invited to sit down on some hard, straight-backed chairs at some steel-legged desks, which

16

scrape the tiled floor, setting my teeth on edge. There is a whiteboard, a computer hard drive on the floor and a flat screen television mounted on the wall.

Cliff, Deputy Principal of the school, addresses us with a welcome message. He seems nervous and unaccustomed to public speaking and bears a striking resemblance to a stork chick. His bird-like twitchy mannerisms and jerky head movements add to the stork chick comparison, as he coughs and sniffs through his prepared speech.

"I'm sure you will find this school a challenge at first, but if you persevere, and we work together… as a team, helping each other, supporting each other, you will find your time here hugely rewarding… and the children will achieve… in their own way, and your efforts will surely bear fruit. You may have to lower the bar, so to speak, in order to build confidence… and eventually, well, the children will achieve… some results."

He ended off with a little bow, which was a cue for Joanne, the principal, to appear in the doorway.

"Good mornin, good mornin. How are we all? Settled in alright, I hope," she smiles brightly making her way to stand in front of the whiteboard, continually scrolling through information on her smart phone.

Joanne was a *South Park* character brought to life; a series of circular shapes for head, including round framed glasses, body, boobs and bum.

We, the new teachers were seated in groups and supplied with felt-tips and big sheets of paper. There was me, Tessa, P.E. Dave, Sandra, Rupert, Tim, and a few others who didn't live in our building. We went round in the compulsory name and brief intro for each person.

"Hello I'm (name). I'm from (country/ town)."

We were then each to say a bit about ourselves. Personally, I find this cringe-worthy and say something short, in order to move on to the next person as quickly as possible. But when it was Tim's turn, he went into a great deal of detail about his life: likes and dislikes; about how he was going to make a difference to the lives of the children at the school; about how he was going to get involved with after school activities and encourage the children to succeed; finishing up with "I play semi-professional football."

The room was suddenly silent as everyone looked at Tim trying to work out if he was joking or not. He sat there serious as anything, thin and pasty with one eye looking at the board, the other trained on something outside the window, both blinking behind thick glasses, which sat, slightly crooked on his bony nose. He had the appearance of someone who could possibly play tiddlywinks, but nothing that involved running around.

In the awkward pause which followed, Dave closed his eyes in silent prayer and I had to hold down explosive giggles that I could feel bubbling up inside. I turned them into a cough, covering my mouth with my hand.

18

"Uh puh-lease," breathed a woman wearing black, sitting next to me; her fingers heavy with gold jewellery, her face heavy with make-up. "This is a total waste of my time," she continued from behind her dark glasses.

This was Salma, a Sicilian Canadian who had been living and teaching in Kuwait for a long, long time. She had accepted the job at the school to get away from an ex-boyfriend at her previous appointment. The situation had turned ugly and she had to make a quick get-away. She had the look of a Mafia mom as she drummed dark red acrylic nails on the table top. She was a year one teacher who would go on to be head of primary.

After the slightly awkward brainstorm session entitled *Problems and Solutions*, we were shown to our classrooms. Mine was down a dimly lit corridor away from the main quad area. I stood at the doorway and looked inside. There were the same psychiatric-ward-blue tiles on the floor and walls and the same grey, utilitarian Formica topped desks and hard chairs that I had been sitting on, in the meeting room. I pondered why we were having our introductory meeting in a room obviously used for containment of violent offenders, but after viewing my own classroom, it dawned on me that it was just a regular classroom. Mine, I was happy to observe, was minus the demonic graffiti.

A flat-screen TV was mounted on the wall. There was a set of shelves, a teacher's desk, a whiteboard, enough chairs and desks for twenty eight children and a computer hard-drive. There was one tatty display board. The only natural light came in through a window which looked down on the quad of the Arabic school next door. This confused my sense of direction for weeks until someone pointed out that it was not the quad in our school.

I could see that my classroom was most definitely not a classroom where children would want to be: it was not a classroom where I wanted to be. I was disheartened by the cold hardness of the learning space. Where was the classroom stuff? The text books, reading books, pictures, wall charts, atlases, dictionaries, globe, map of the world, scissors, glue, whiteboard pens, whiteboard magnets, mini whiteboards, wall-planner, blutac, tape, felt-tips, markers, stapler, staples, hole-punch, plain white paper, coloured paper, coloured card, rug, cushions for the reading corner, puzzles, board games, counters, rulers, a clock?

It occurred to me that we were expected to create a learning environment out of thin air. A cloud of procrastination suddenly descended. I went in search of Tessa to see how she was getting on.

I found her in the basement, in a cave-like room which had a small narrow window up high at the top of the wall opposite the door. On the wall on the right, at head height was a crude painting of a giant orange flower with a thick green stalk and large dark green leaves - the sort of painting that was supposed to 'cheer things up', but actually had the opposite effect.

"I found this," she said, demonstrating a glove puppet of man with a black moustache, smoking a cigar.

There was a metal trunk, large enough for a body, which was open in the middle of the otherwise empty room. Tessa was going through the contents.

"Most of this stuff is shit," she said, pulling out a broken box of *Snakes and Ladders*, which was empty.

She had been told that each teacher from the previous year had one of these trunks to store their stuff in. All I had to do was to find out which teachers were not returning and nab their stuff, before any of the other new teachers figured this out.

I was reinvigorated by this information, quickly finding out from previous teachers the names of those who were not coming back. Then I scurried round the classrooms, raiding metal trunks in a frenzy of stealing. In one afternoon, I found most of the things I needed and some things I didn't need at all, but grabbed 'just in case'. At the end of the day, my classroom was filled with useful stuff for teaching. My mood elevated and I felt quietly confident I could pull a classroom together from all these bits I had found.

My classroom piracy also gave me the opportunity for a good look around. The layout of the school was a labyrinth and you could tell who was new by the way they wandered around with a slightly worried expression of the lost. There are three floors of classrooms: lower primary and early years occupying the basement; primary school occupying classes on ground, first and second floors; secondary mostly up on the third with some of their classrooms down on the first. The corridors are narrow and would regularly clog with loud, shouting children, fighting their way between lessons, but I didn't know that then. In those early days before the start of term everything was quiet, the way there is calm before a storm.

Sandra, who still didn't have a contract as head of learning support, had volunteered to shift books from a storage room to the library. Some Sri Lankan school labourers were enlisted to do the carting. It was a simple job of moving boxes.

"Where are you going?" she asked, as the last of her helpers exited the storage room.

"We have break now," he said.

"But we haven't started," reasoned Sandra.

"We have break and come in some time," he responded with a friendly smile.

"Ok then, ten minutes," she conceded.

"Yes miss."

Half an hour later, Sandra was still rounding up her work force.

"Right, well, we have to take all these boxes to the library downstairs," she explained.

The men looked around at the boxes of books and murmured to each other in Tamil.

"What's the problem?" she asked, trying to sound sympathetic.

"The men say the box too heavy. They can't take," said the spokesperson.

"You haven't even tried to lift them yet. How do you know they're too heavy?"

The men shuffled about shaking their heads and muttering.

"Look," said Sandra. "I can lift it." And she demonstrated by lifting one of the larger boxes.

"See, it's fine," she smiled broadly, nodding encouragement.

The men reluctantly picked up a box each and with much grunting and groaning, followed Sandra to the lift which took them down to the basement and the library. When they arrived, the men put down their boxes on the floor and sat on them with audible sighs and moans. They hung their heads and wiped their foreheads on their shirt sleeves.

"We very tired miss," was the reply when Sandra questioned what they were doing.

"Well, there are a few more boxes to bring down. Come on, it won't take long," she said trying not to lose her cool.

She had only just stepped through the door of the library, on her way back to the lift, when one of the men threw a punch at another worker. There was shouting and a scuffle and another punch and then a kick and it seemed as if all the men were involved in a full scale brawl.

Sandra felt powerless to intervene, so stood by to allow the fire of fisticuffs to burn itself out.

"Can we continue now?" she said after a few minutes, as the men still breathing heavily, straightened their clothing and retrieved lost shoes.

Back in the lift, she pressed the button to return to the upper floor. The door closed, there was a bang and the lights went out.

Sandra fumbled in her bag for her phone and turned it on. She found the emergency button and pressed it forcefully a number of times.

"Shit!"

Of course, there was no phone coverage inside the lift, so they just stood waiting in the dark.

Later, when she was retelling this tale over a glass of wine, she said at this point that she nearly lost it.

"I could feel myself getting really panicky, like really claustrophobic. If any of those bleeders laid a hand on me I would have let them have it. I mean, I wouldn't have been able to stop myself. I swear, it was the most trapped I have ever been." She was laughing when she was telling me, but I knew she wasn't at the time.

Rupert had found his office which was handily located at the end of my corridor. I popped my head in to see how his day was going. He was trying to make sense of envelopes and ring-binders that were packed with paper and stacked on a huge conference table, which was way too big for the size of the room.

"I'm not sure what I'm supposed to do with this lot," he said, slightly bemused with a little laugh. "There's some really sensitive information here, about the kids and it's just been left."

Clearly, his predecessor hadn't been very thorough with filing, or had just scarpered at the end of the previous term, leaving the office in a mountainous disarray.

"I just want to put it all in the bin."

Simon was barely coping in his science lab upstairs on the third floor. To try and steer away from moaning, I commented that he had really good natural light, compared to Tessa and me, and a view from his window.

"And that's all I got," he said in his usual grumpy way. "There's not even one Bunsen burner and no chemicals! How am I supposed to teach science without Bunsen burners?" He was shaking his head while he said this and putting up laminated posters of the periodic table. I could tell he was seeing the glass as half empty. Looking around, I had nothing to say that would make the situation better, so I left.

Dave had spent his first day hiding in the P.E. staffroom, trying to avoid Tim, who I found in his empty classroom just sitting, staring at the wall.

"You OK?" I said, feeling like I should sound like I cared.

"Yeah," he replied. "I'm just planning what I'm going to do with my classroom."

"Cool," I said about to leave and continue foraging.

"Yeah, it's going to be great. Yeah. I'm going to make this bit over here a pirate ship. Then over there is going to be a jungle with animals and things. Yeah."

"Well, good luck with that," I said, knowing in my heart that none of this grand vision was ever going to materialise. I left Tim still sitting in his classroom, staring at the wall.

By the end of the prep week my classroom was nowhere near ready, I was not prepared and I only had a sketchy idea of what I was going to do with the children in the first few days. It was now Thursday. The children were to start the following Sunday. I had so much to do I didn't know where to begin. A mild panic had made a home in my gut. I was contemplating my list of priorities when Joanne called an emergency meeting downstairs in the theatre.

"It is possibly no surprise for you to know that we are still waiting for some teachers to arrive," she said. "So, I have decided to postpone the opening of school for another week. This will give the newly arrived teachers time to get their classroom organised, and give the teachers who are organised time to sort out the classrooms for the teachers who aren't here yet."

There was some low muttering from the auditorium as the teaching staff shuffled off. I couldn't believe my luck. A whole extra week to prepare! The gods of primary teachers were smiling.

A few days later, I experienced a wholehearted sense of satisfaction as I surveyed my classroom. Colourful pin boards with borders graced the walls, ready to display the wonderful work my children would produce that year. There was a map of Great Britain for the introductory topic *Everything British*; labelled plastic bins containing, as yet unnamed, exercise books for English, Maths, Science and Topic. There were two shelving units with trays for each child to store their classroom items; a globe; a map of the world (minus Israel, which had been blacked out with a permanent marker); several stacks of text books for each subject; some cubby-holes with useful things I would need for my teaching practice, including coloured paper, plain paper, lolly sticks, building blocks; a clock with movable hands and a variety of games and puzzles for quiet play. There was even a comfy book corner with cushions where children could choose a book they liked and read it, intent on making sense of the pictures and words, delighting in their progress.

Ah yes, I had created a learning environment for the children to thrive in and, like a magician, I had pulled all this together out of nothing. In my imagination, parents would greet me at the end of the year, teary eyed and grateful for the wonderful gift of education their child had received in my class. They would present me with beautifully wrapped expensive gifts, which I would at first refuse, but then concede after the remonstrations of the emotional parents.

"Please, please you must. We beg of you," they will say and I, with the utmost humility, will graciously accept with the words "Really, this isn't necessary. I was just doing my job."

Downstairs in early years, a shipment of resources had arrived. It was meant to have been delivered sometime during the summer holiday, so now we had to deal with it in what would have been the first week of school. I joined in the job of checking the contents against the packing slips. Baby elephant-sized cardboard cartons were piled up in a haphazard fashion; some opened, some not. A few other teachers were already busy with the task, working in pairs: one pulling out contents and counting, the other quizzically scanning the list to look for a match.

I opened one of the cartons, which was full of sand timers; different colours to denote different times, from fifteen seconds to ten minutes.

"This can't be right". I counted one hundred and forty five. These sand timers were left in their box, in a corridor for some time and teachers were urged to claim them for their classrooms. The box sat side by side with other boxes containing three thousand English text books for the secondary department. This was an admin botch up where, instead of thirty books each, in a successive progression completing a full course from one to ten, three thousand copies of book one had been ordered.

Midway through the year the boxes, still containing a good number of the original one hundred and forty five sand timers, and the useless secondary English text books, were shifted to a store room with other unclaimed equipment and forgotten about.

The equipment, obviously ordered by the previous year's staff who had some plan for it all, was varying in terms of quality and usefulness. The expressions on the faces of people unpacking were a mixture of incredulity, surprise and a childlike delight. Part of the shipment was a host of classroom hardware, including play furniture for kindergarten, paint and printing ink for the art department, little polystyrene balls to fill beanbags, metre rules, around two hundred small mirrors. And ten sacks of sand for the sandpit, imported from England. I looked around to see if anyone else had found this funny. Apparently not.

3

This is tomorrow calling

One of the things that was glaringly clear to me when I arrived at the school, was the sad lack of tech-hardware. My classroom was furnished with hard grey chairs and desks for the children that fitted perfectly with my idea of pre-Glasnost, cold-war Russia. There was a teacher's desk and chair, of the same grey Formica and steel construction; a flat screen television, mounted on the wall, which had the potential to be connected to a grey ancient hard drive, the size of two breeze blocks, on the floor by a wall, where there were two power sockets. There was no keyboard or mouse or monitor.

On inspection, my classroom was typical of all the classrooms at the school. It wasn't as if someone in the-powers-that-be forgot to put the rest of my computer in my room; the bits just weren't there. Anywhere.

I may be old fashioned, but in my mind a functioning computer must have the following components, 1) a hard drive, 2) a keyboard, 3) a mouse, and 4) a monitor. As far as I could tell, I only had one of these things. Then I learned from a colleague, a returning teacher, that we were supposed to use the wall-mounted TV as a monitor. Mmmmmmm. OK.

Considering Kuwait bills itself as a forward-thinking country - you only have to read the Kuwaiti Airways in-flight magazine to discover how Kuwaitis see themselves; tech savvy, sophisticated, label-wearing, brand-orientated, latest-model-car-owner, ritzy-glitzy hotel stayer, designer-flashy - there is a distinct lack of technology available at school.

There wasn't even a photocopier available for staff to use. We had to take anything we wanted copied to the photocopy room, where it would be done for us by the long suffering Trishna, who repeatedly complained about her sore fingers, from entering digits on the photocopier keypad. Teachers weren't allowed to touch the copiers, which was a little frustrating. And bizarrely enough, there weren't any printers for teachers' use. Management had them, and luckily for me, Rupert was happy to let me print out anything I wanted, in his office. The accepted premise is that teachers buy their own printers, but I flatly refuse.

Everyone in Kuwait, it seems, is well connected to the World Wide Web through a smart phone, iPad and computer. The street billboards advertise a range of tech products and service providers with mega download deals and uber-fast, no-waiting-for-any-time-at-all upload promises. But with all this connectivity and access to global information, Kuwait is heavily censored and there is the feeling that no-one really knows what is going on.

Across the road from the school there is the Sultan's Centre supermarket and a collection of ugly cuboid buildings, which house a number of little shops. These tiny businesses are mostly phone shops, selling all the latest gadgetry and devices, accessories and connections. The brand names shout out from signage and posters, one after another, side by side, and I wonder how they can all be surviving, as they all sell the same things.

People here seem to be consumed by new communication technology like nowhere else on earth. They are super consumers. They can afford the latest of everything and they love to show off the new and shiny things they have bought. These comtech gadgets are a measure of status, to make your life complete, inspire admiration and make people want to be your friend.

One of the huge dichotomies of this Arab state is that even though the population of Kuwait is well-connected and know about the world outside, they are still OK about sending their children to a school with its glaring deficits in general learning environment, school facilities and comtech hardware. There is no wireless internet and the connection that is available is slow and regularly down. Some teachers relent and buy their own mobile modems. I flatly refuse.

On *News Tuesday*, an informal opportunity for children to practise speaking English before the planned lessons start, the subject of shopping comes up a lot.

"Last Saturday I go…."

"went"

"I went with my family to *Xcite* and I buy…"

"Bought"

"Yes, I bought iPhone 6 and the new Minecraft."

"Great. Thanks Mohammed. Did anyone do anything else apart from shopping? (Waits for a response.) No? OK, well, if you think of something you would like to share, just put up your hand." (Silence.)

The children in my class can't quite believe that I don't have a smart phone and they laugh raucously when I show them Little Blackie, my old trusty Nokia 100, circa ages ago.

"Why you no have, Miss?" Abdullah asks, trying to understand how I can still be alive.

So anyway, before the children arrive I have to somehow piece together my classroom computer out of nothing. And that is when I went snooping.

First stop, to find an I.C.T. room: upstairs in the secondary department, I found one. Mick, the I.C.T. teacher, a middle aged, chubby Irishman was lying on his back, under one the desks, his hands full of a tangle of wire and cables.

"You'll be lucky to find anything useful like a monitor," he replied with a laugh, when I inquired. "They're tight bastards, y'know. I don't even have what I need to teach the secondary curriculum. Just look at these things," he said, hands still full of wire spaghetti, nodding at the ancient computers around the room. "They're dinosaurs." He ended off with a resigned chuckle as his head disappeared under the table.

After a bit more wandering and meeting more teachers, I returned to my classroom and noticed a door next to mine, with a sign which read 'Marking Room'. In the marking room there are four computer desks with actual computers; hard drives, mouses, keyboards and monitors. Expectantly, I press each power-on button and wait as the screens flicker awake. Computers one and four work straight away, but computers two and three just show an error message.

Carefully, I unraveled the cables and unplugged a monitor, mouse and keyboard from one of the dysfunctional machines and installed them into my classroom. Then, I thought, I would go and order replacements from tech-support, where ever that was. Job done. It's not like I was stealing anything; I was merely borrowing until the end of the year when I will put it all back. Tidily.

I made inquiries about comtech ordering with one of the returning teachers, and was directed to the technical support office in the maze of the basement. It was like a movie set of narrow, poorly lit corridors. There was no signage and abandoned, broken furniture lay dotted about, while fluorescent lighting blinked intermittently on and off. As I turned a corner, I heard voices and poked my head round a door. "Hello, is this technical support?"

To my relief it was, and a friendly Indian man took my details and wrote some particulars on a post-it. Then he told me it was very unlikely that my request would come to anything, as only year leaders and management had monitors, and having one was a mark of status, and if you were a mere teacher, you would be forgetting your station in life. I thanked him for his kind words and scurried back to my classroom.

Judging by the lack of other comtech in school, I suppose if a teacher did want a monitor or in fact anything for the classroom, the expectation was; if you need something, go buy it yourself. Again, I flatly refused.

Who knew if the items I ordered would ever arrive? I didn't really care. I had found what I needed to make my computer go and when I turned the machine on and it actually worked, I felt a wave of success wash over me. I had a fully functioning computer. I could now do my job.

Weeks passed. The routines of school became less manic and the glitches in the weekly time-table were ironed out. I wrote lessons plans on my computer, which I typed and filed on the school shared drive, then printed out and photocopied. I researched resources on the internet which were downloaded and stored on the desktop and relevant YouTube clips were shown to the children on the flat screen TV to illustrate teaching points. (YouTube was a site that had been blocked by the school, but there are ways around annoyances like blocked internet sites.) Everything was going quite well.

One afternoon, as I was planning lessons for the following day, Myrtle, Deputy Head of Primary, popped her head in.

"Joanne wants you to put the monitor back," she said.

"Haha," I laughed out loud, thinking she was joking. I then explained that I had ordered one and just as soon as it arrived I would most definitely return the borrowed monitor to the marking room. Then followed up with "You know those computers don't work," indicating the marking room with a nod of the head. "I've only borrowed it," trying not to sound guilty.

She wasn't joking.

Weeks pass. I am trying to be on top of all things teachery from classroom behaviour management, which seems to be filling most of my day, to individual reading records and wall displays. One day, I get a visit from Rupert.

"Joanne wants you to put the monitor back," he says.

"Ah, yes, well those computers…" and I explain again the monitor scenario. He leaves and I carry on doing my job.

At the end of the week I get a visit from Joanne herself.

"Put the monitor back," she says in her nasally Liverpudlian accent. Then, before I get up from my desk to explain, she has disappeared out the door and round the corner. I just get a glimpse of her backside, as I yell after her "But the computers don't work!"

The computers in the marking room still hadn't been fixed and my monitor, the one on order, still had not arrived.

The last day before the half term holidays, I was summoned into Joanne's office.

"Sit down, Miss," she said, indicating a low sofa by the wall. She and Cliff were perched, each on high-backed, power-trippy office chairs. I knew what this was going to be about. It was the high noon show down. Monitorgate. I relaxed back into the sofa in an attempt to show I was not the least bit intimidated.

"You have been asked to put the monitor back….a number of times, and still you have not complied," she continued.

"But," I began.

"You will get your turn to speak in a moment, but first I must issue this written warning."

Bloody hell. I wasn't expecting that.

I knew, then and there, that my suspicions were correct. That this was not a school at all, but some kind of weird, post-apocalyptic parallel universe that I had somehow fallen into: an Orwellian world with no feasible logic or common sense. From then on, I kept my head down, tried my best to operate under the radar, become invisible, do my job, then get out with my sanity intact.

I put the monitor back.

Back at the Ivory Tower there is still no internet access. We had been promised a connection at the school accommodation, as part of the pay package and weeks into the term, it had still not been installed. I believe this was because management were hoping the teachers would give up and buy their own. I flatly refused.

A handy man called round to hook up the flat screen TV at the Ivory Tower, but I declined his kind offer. I figure that television is crap in most places in the world and I'd rather not give myself the option of flicking it on. I didn't want to get sucked into a telly watching habit here, preferring to keep a Zen-like peace at in my Zen-like home. Besides, if I wanted to watch something on TV, I could always make it a social occasion and call round to visit the neighbours.

Tessa had the TV tuned in at her place and a flat mate who had it turned on all the time. Marjorie, a little, round, sweet, silver-haired grandmother who wore glasses, arrived from South Africa and now occupied the other room in Tessa's apartment. She was sweet and gentle until she was in her year one classroom, then she became a fire-breathing dragon. She had a thin stick in her class to use, not to beat the children, but to hit the tables in order to get their attention. Sandra confiscated the stick and informed management that there was some possible psychological intimidation going on. Nothing was done and Marjorie acquired another stick.

Tessa, who was a health-conscious, vegetarian, animal lover, put up with Marjorie, the chain smoking, meat-eater, telly-watcher. Tessa spent more and more time in other people's apartments.

Simon was still undecided about whether to stay or go. He had been furiously applying for secondary science teacher jobs, anywhere, as the inadequacies of the science department continued to reveal themselves. Not only, were there no Bunsen burners or even a gas supply, there were no chemicals or ventilation system for doing

38

chemistry experiments, even if there were chemicals to do them with. As the term progressed, he became more and more intense and difficult to be around. Then the day came when he was made an offer by a school in Rome.

It was one of Dave's favourite games to get Simon's internal hamster wheel spinning.

"So, do you think you're going to take that job?" asked Dave one afternoon, while Tessa and I were over watching a FIFA match on the telly. We shot him a 'what the fuck?' look, while he was trying to suppress potentially explosive giggles into his mug.

But Simon's dilemma had deepened with his obvious bromance with Dave.

"I just don't know, Big Man," he said shaking his head, unaware of the hilarity in the room. He looked longingly at his muscley flat mate, while brushing popcorn crumbs off his t-shirt, licking his fingers then wiping them on the arm of the couch. "I just don't know."

The automated world of computing admin had only half happened at school. We had been asked to use temporary paper registers because the official paper registers were still at the printers: it was like being back in the seventies. While teachers in other schools in the contemporary world, kept a record of present, late and absent children, on an easy-to-use computer programme; we had to write out the names of kids in class, according to the class list handed out at the beginning of the year. This class list, as I found out, was not cast in stone and served as more of a fluid guide to who was going to turn up.

Subsequently, my attempt at listing children in alphabetical order neatly on a page was thwarted, as I crossed out names of children who weren't in my class and wrote in names of children who had turned up, but were not on the list. There was inevitably some confusion and it was a good few weeks into the term, when I realised I had three Mohammeds in class and not just the two, written on the list.

When the official paper registers did arrive, I noticed with a smile, the interesting numbering in the margin, that went 21, 22, 23, 21, 25. Apparently, everyone was aware of this error, but nothing had been done to fix it. Similarly, the paper mark book, a useful document for teachers to note down children's test marks, completed homework, etc, was labelled *Mare Book*. Another example of 'it is what it is'. I had learned, and was careful to write all names of the children in my class in pencil, just in case.

I voiced my concerns about the lack of equipment and general inefficiency to Olga, a teacher from Romania, who had been at the school for ten years, that maybe, the school was not up to standard and how the hell was she still here?

"This is not the worst school," she explained ominously with a heavily Eastern European accent. "I have been to the worst school. At least here, there are books."

Despite my best efforts at dropping hints, the lavish gifts for the teacher at the end of the year, did not materialise. Even though the children laughed openly at Little Blackie and my lack of smart, hand-held connection, still they did not furnish me with updated technology on their departure. I mentioned phones a great deal in those last few weeks, and even joked that I would kindly take a tired old iPhone 5 off their hands now that they had the very sleek and up to the minute iPhone 6, that they continually bragged about. I even told my class, in a haha jokey way, that whoever bought me a well-thought out, expensive gift for the end of year, would get A's in all subjects, haha. But, no, the hinting went unheeded and when my class was dismissed for the last time, there were no colourful, ribbon wrapped, presentation boxes gracing my table. Not one.

4

Teaching

The hardest thing I found about living in Kuwait was adjusting to the Islamic working week - Sunday to Thursday. I never did get used to it. Every cell in my body would scream 'No!' at the five thirty alarm on a Sunday morning. It took all my strength to heave myself out of my lovely bed to get ready for school by seven. The misery of the Sunday start should have been off-set by the joy of the early finish on Thursday, but this never really cut it. The psychological and cultural weight of Sunday being a fun day was too robustly imbedded in my western being. So in my bleary and slightly stunned state, I waited for my class on the first day of term.

The children turned up in dribs and drabs in those early weeks, which was a blessing because the school was still lacking a whole lot of classroom teachers. Everything was a bit of a scramble as class lists, time-tables and teachers were juggled and re-jigged. It was sometime after the mid-term break when I finally had a full class. Families were still travelling for summer, I was told. This general lackadaisical approach to school and attendance was to be a continual battle.

The level of ability was much lower than I had anticipated and I quickly had to adapt my planning. My six months of supply teaching different age groups in South London had given me a fair idea of what year four children were capable of, but the children in my class displayed gaping holes in their skills and knowledge across the board. And they had very short attention spans. This was largely due, I assumed, to a lack of English language.

Being in a room full of children is like being in a cage with wild animals - you can't let down your guard for one minute, otherwise you will be eaten alive. This I felt was doubly true of the children in my class. They had no idea of how to be 'at school' and they didn't seem to know what my role was in the classroom. I felt that they regarded me as one of their maids: someone who there to pander to their needs and clear up after them; someone who lets them do exactly what they want.

In Kuwait, and other Arab states, it is not unusual for families to employ maids to look after the children. Out in public, you see families at restaurants and malls, the mums and dads often sitting at a table chatting on their cell phones or busy on their iPads, while the imported maids, usually from a South East Asian countries, in their maid's uniform, tend to the tyrannical offspring. The boys especially, treated like little princes, are allowed to demand, shout and lash-out at the hired help, with no apparent parental intervention.

There are horror stories of slavery, where girls from poor families are sold to Kuwaitis, to work seven days a week in appalling conditions with absolutely no rights at all. In fact, if a family is not happy with their maid, they can return her in exchange for another, no problem.

This means that the reject is now unemployed and unemployable because who wants a used maid? So, with this in mind, the imported 'help' will put up with poor treatment and keep their mouth shut.

There are supposed to be guidelines in place to protect imported workers and the agencies are obliged to ensure the safety of the maids, but with the seemingly unlimited human product, who is really going to care enough to follow this up? If a woman is problematic she is can be easily replaced. There are plenty more desperate poor women who are just grateful for a job and a roof over their head, however shitty the conditions. In a country where women are second class citizens anyway, the immigrant maid is the bottom of the heap.

Once, as I was searching for the Indian visa office in Fahaheel, I found myself on one of the upper floors in one of the mall buildings. I turned a corner in a stairwell and was confronted with a queue of women who looked as though they had just arrived from the airport. They sat together on the stairs and along the corridors with their bags and bundles, waiting to be signed up to one of many 'employment agencies' that occupied offices on that floor. This is where they paid a fee for a placement into a household. The young women, wearing clothes denoting country of origin were quietly, patiently waiting their turn.

I felt the weight of my cultural currency: the sheer luck that I had been born into the western world, speaking a language that was internationally recognised as global, and was in the position to trade it for cash, made me at once hugely grateful and painfully humble. A twist of fate and I could easily have been one of these women waiting to be sold into slavery.

As a direct result of no parental boundaries, the children's behaviour in class was nightmarish. The boys' being far worse than the girls', which meant I had to use the handful of girls available, in a class made up mostly of boys, as violence buffers in the seating arrangements. While I tried to get attention, so I could deliver instruction, the children continually talked to each other in Arabic and used things, such as bits of erasers, as missiles. They tore corners from their books and wrote abusive notes. They pushed and elbowed whenever possible. They purposely dropped pencils, rulers, pencil cases, in fact anything at all, on the floor to cause disruption and chaos. It was extremely difficult to maintain a noise level that was conducive to learning. I tried to implement the 'no fail' rules and routines that I had learned in teacher training - focusing on positive behaviour and praising those who were on task and paying attention. This had worked a treat in my final practicum, and I tried to remember the simple psychology while supply teaching in London. But here, in this class…

"Stop!.....And again stop!........Just waiting for five more people to stop what they are doing……Thank you everyone who is listening…..Still waiting…..Hold your hands like this, then you won't be tempted to fiddle……Omar, look at me…….and Sultan, Ahmed, Shahad, Mohammed, Saud, Abdullah stop what you are doing……..Still waiting……." And so it went on as the clock ticked away the day.

I became the shouty teacher.

I sent children outside. I sent children for time-out in my buddy class. I sent children to Mr Rupert's office, which, thankfully, was just at the end of the corridor. I wrote notes home to parents. I filled out behaviour incident sheets. I made children miss break/ lunch/ P.E. (the high-light of their week). At one point, I had eleven boys on daily behaviour report, which meant meetings with parents, sometimes with the help of a translator, signing of agreements to try and improve behaviour, so that the children could focus on learning something.

The parents, on the whole, were accommodating and supported our efforts to get a change in attitude, which would, fingers crossed, lead to a change in behaviour. Although, I did stupidly give my number to one mother (oh how I regretted that) who would call me at night to ask why her little darling was missing his break and how could I possibly be so cruel as to deny him P.E.? I didn't answer her calls and she began to ambush me on the way to class in the morning. My comment was always courteous and clear.

Me: He is missing his break because he is fighting with the other boys.

The mum: He is good boy. Other boy is bad. Look at him. (Boy looks up at his mother with the glowing smile of a saint.)He is good boy. He loves you too much miss.

Me: When he shows he can behave properly – line up without pushing, sit quietly without talking, stand with the others without fighting – then he can play.

46

The mum: He cannot miss break. He sick. The doctor say he must eat.

I look at the over-weight child thinking it would do no harm for him to skip a meal.

Me: I'm sure he will be good today (I lie).

The mum: Enshaallah!

The school trip to Kidzania was coming up and I saw this treat as an opportunity for some behavioural leverage.

"So, does everyone understand that from now until our trip next week, I will be noticing you being 'good'. We all know what that means now. Anyone who still doesn't know, will not be going."

There were silent nods and pairs of large, innocent eyes stared up at me, dewy with grace and goodness.

Thirty seconds later, in the corridor outside the classroom a fight had broken out.

"You, you, you and you will not be going to Kidzania!" I bellowed.

The night before the outing my phone is ringing. It's Sultan's mum.

"Please, please, I begging you, my son he cry. He so sad. My mother's heart, it breaks. I cry. Why he cannot go?" she wails.

"He can't go because 1) I can't trust him to behave properly in a public place and 2) I told all the children that anyone who cannot behave properly in school, would not be going. If he is allowed to go, that directly undermines my authority."

"But he cry!"

"I'm sorry, but maybe he will learn from this. Enshaallah."

The morning of the trip, the father of one of the other excluded boys comes to see me.

"He is in the car and I say to him, I will talk to your teacher and maybe she will say 'yes' you can go to Kidzania."

"No. Absolutely not."

"But he is sad. He is in the car. He cry. You say he cannot go and he cry."

"Please talk to your son about his behaviour and make him understand that fighting is not allowed at all, anywhere."

It was becoming clear that there seemed to be no linking of behaviour to punishment in the children's or some of the parents' minds. The children couldn't seem to make that connection and take responsibility for their actions. All my energy seemed to be used up in managing behaviour and made life at school exhausting hard work.

At the end of each day, I collapsed on the sofa in our lounge where Tessa and I would have a lengthy debrief of classroom events. We had developed a daily ritual, a form of decompression, where we had a good laugh telling each other of the comedy highlights *du jour*.

"They don't seem to be able to hold information in their heads," Tessa said exasperated, one hand on her forehead as she lay on the couch, staring up at the ceiling, like someone in therapy. "I have labelled everything. I repeat it. I hold up what they need to bring in, 'your pencil case, your glue, not your lunchbox, not your Arabic book', and still they don't get it. They just don't think! Then, just before break, Hamad opened his mango juice and I swear it exploded! Up the wall. Everywhere. There's even mango juice on the ceiling! And at that moment, and poor Mohammed was standing in front of him, and he wears glasses, and he was covered in it, like a cartoon. He had to take his glasses off to see! Bless him. The whole class was stunned into silence. Then Hamad said 'the maid, she do for me,' like it was the maid's fault he was covered in mango juice!"

The school, like most schools in Kuwait, follows the British curriculum. It is billed as an international school, implying that the school caters for families of people from a variety of English speaking countries, who are living and working here. Not so. The school is very much a local school with a role of mostly Arabic speakers whose families want the quality of education available to children in the U.K.

And here lies the glaring contention which was at the heart of a good percentage of the problems I faced as a teacher in Kuwait - to deliver the British curriculum in English to Arabic children in Kuwait. The children were lacking in, not only English, but the cultural cues and background that British people just take for granted. I was using books with illustrations of rabbits, foxes, trees and grass, with streams and lakes and hedgehogs, butterflies and ladybirds – the imagery of the

British countryside. The Kuwaiti kids had no clue about these things. I had to choose carefully and make content as relevant as I could.

The children in my year four class, had problems with the most basic classroom etiquette. I had to rewind learning and start again from the beginning: how to raise your hand when you have something to say and not call out "Miss, Miss, Miss"; how to write the date and underline it with a ruler; how to hold a pencil, in some cases; how to walk calmly in a line, one behind the other (this, alas, they would never master).

It was clear after a while that, on top of the obvious language and cultural barriers, at least half the class had severe learning difficulties. For some children, these difficulties were a direct result of an ever decreasing Kuwaiti gene pool.

I had never met an inbred child before coming to Kuwait, but when you meet a few, you recognise certain subtle traits – something not quite right around the eyes, a vagueness, a social ineptness, a slack mouth, the way the child moves around or just sits and stares blankly. There is just a feeling that the child is 'not all there'.

I had a few F.L.K.s (Funny Looking Kids) in my class. These children's mummies and daddies were probably first cousins or closely related in some other way I would rather not think about. The idea of inter-family pairing being, of course, to keep the blood line pure and wealth within the clan.

One boy was so impaired he could barely speak cohesive words in Arabic or English: he made sounds like a wookie. He could not hold a pencil to write; he could not recognise numbers in a sequence; he could not sound out letters of the alphabet; he could only understand simple commands from me if I was extra slow and clear. His mum came to see me after the first round of assessments. I tried to remain positive.

Me: (Nodding and smiling.) Saad is a good boy. He tries his best. He is always smiling.

The mum, nodding and smiling says something to the interpreter.

The interpreter: She wants to know how is he academically.

Me: (Nodding and smiling.) He does not find things easy. He struggles. But he tries.

What could I say? This child needs help. He should be in a special school. He should at least be in an Arabic speaking school. He is barely at KG level.

He was not the only one.

Parent interaction varied widely. Some parents of the children in my class I never met, while others had to be shaken off, avoided or out witted with me running out to bogus meetings at the end of the school day. One parent, when I told him his son was one of the ring-leaders of violent behaviour, enthusiastically shared with me a snippet of wisdom that he had acquired from a conference for project managers. I was backed into a corner.

"'First, there is storm, then there is form, then there is norm, and THEN there is perform!' This is how it is in my job as well," he explained with huge gestures to illustrate each phase of the learning continuum. "People have to come through the chaos and then settle down before they can PERFORM!" he almost sang this last word as if he were on stage giving an encore.

I appreciated the message, but looking back, I don't believe my class ever left the 'storm' phase.

In the light of the language obstacles, I decided early on to keep lessons as hands-on and interactive as possible. But it's the hands-on, interactive lessons that leave the door to possible fuck-ups, wide open. One such lesson was for science, an experiment to discover which common kitchen solids are soluble.

In the introductory lesson the children brain-stormed ideas of solids that they might find in the kitchen that they could bring into class to test. I wrote their ideas on the whiteboard. Then they were grouped together according to mixed ability, and I gave them time to discuss which items each group member was to bring for the following lesson. They wrote a note in their homework diaries as a reminder.

"So, you will each bring the solid you have chosen in a plastic jar like this with a screw top lid," I explained, holding up my demo jar containing a couple of table-spoons of salt in the bottom. I tipped the jar upside-down to show how secure the lid was, and banged the edge of the table to show how plastic was safe and wouldn't shatter on impact, unlike glass, as we had discussed.

I then went round the room asking all the children what they were bringing to school for the science experiment. They each said out loud what they were going to bring.

"Sugar."

"Coffee."

"Tea."

And so on.

There were a couple of discrepancies, but I believed naively that we had them ironed out by the end of the session, and that there was an understanding that the next lesson we would be conducting a scientific experiment.

The day of the experiment was two days later. Needless to say, only a handful of children had brought solids from their kitchen to test. I had anticipated this and was prepared with salt, sugar, porridge oats from home, plus coffee and a teabag from the staffroom.

One girl, a perpetual overachiever, had brought three jars which were carefully labelled with the contents. I praised her diligence and awarded star cards. She beamed while the others scowled and muttered.

Another girl had brought her salt and sugar in small decorative glass jars in a glittery presentation gift bag with tags which read "I love the scence (science)!", "I love the miss!"

Another of my sensible girls had six labeled, zip-locked bags each containing salt, sugar, coffee, tea, flour and drinking chocolate. I made a show of my appreciation and awarded star cards accordingly. She had not brought any containers, so I asked her to see if she could find some empty water bottles around the school to use.

No-one else in class had brought anything to contribute to the experiment apart from one boy who had brought in a kilo bag of sugar. Clearly he had missed the point.

We cleared the tables of books and pencil cases, and I spoke briefly about how this was a science experiment and that observation and noticing what was going on, was key. I reminded them of the terminology and the vocabulary that we were using – dissolving, solid, liquid, soluble, etc.

I said that now they were all scientists with an important job to do. They had to notice what happened to the contents of the jars when they added water and then notice what happened after thirty minutes. They then had to say why a reaction happened or didn't happen.

I drew a table with three columns on the whiteboard with these headings and the list of solids we were testing in the jars.

On the command 'start', all hell broke loose. The children shouted at each other in a cacophony of Arabic and water was spilled on the tables and floor. I roamed the class trying to calm the situation and encourage scientific study.

"Miiiiiiiss, Abdullah and Mohammed, they fight," said a sensible girl, holding an empty jar showing a plastic lid that had been over-screwed and had shattered, allowing the contents to flood onto the floor. I looked over to where the fracas was taking place and saw a sizable puddle of sweetened water between two boys who were still at each other. I stepped between them with giant strides, ordering them to sit by themselves on opposite sides of the room.

"And you are missing lunch!" I bellowed.

I asked one of the sensible girls to find a maid with a mop to come and help with the cleanup. With that situation dealt with I surveyed the classroom landscape.

As expected, about half the class were sitting, chatting; a few were flicking bits of erasers at other children's heads; a few were shaking jars vigorously (I had expressly told them not to); a few were scribbling on pieces of paper that had been torn from their science exercise books; three boys saw an opportunity to chase each other round the tables. I ignored all of this and focused on the children that seemed genuinely interested in the science in the jars.

While I was delighting in a hands-on teaching moment, a boy shot past me and started retching into the rubbish bin, next to the door.

"He drink!" a sensible girl informed me. Trying to take this in, another boy pushed past and threw up next to the retching individual.

"STOP!" I shouted. "What is going on?"

Most of the class eventually stopped what they were doing and were looking at me for what was coming next, but there was a tussle and some shouting as someone said "Ala, he do it Miss!"

The kilo bag of sugar was spilling out of a large tear in the plastic as Ala held the bag, its contents forming a sugar mountain on the table top, which spilled over the edge, causing a sugar waterfall to the floor, where it was engulfed into the sugary lake from the previous incident.

As a result of silliness and lack of thinking during the science lesson, eight children were on lunch-time detention, and I had to write notes to parents about potential dangers of ingesting scientific test samples. I admit this was clearly my fault for not being specific enough in my instruction, as I had not directly said the words "Do not drink the experiment."

Amusing teaching anecdotes abound. Every day some incident stops me in mid flow and I stand for a moment wondering if a child is testing me or if they really are 'that thick'. It made me wonder what the future held for these children.

In response to the question, "What do you want to do when you leave school?" most of the boys replied "engineer," and the girls replied "doctor". I don't know if they had the slightest idea what they were saying or what these jobs entailed. Maybe they just heard the words somewhere or were told by their parents that this was the plan.

In secondary, Helen had different replies to the question. Apparently, all the children in years eight, nine, ten and eleven had no intention of getting a job. They were all going to be successful bloggers and spend their time tweeting the world about their interesting lives.

Downstairs, Tessa's class was learning about things that float and things that sink. Tessa had prepared a practical lesson providing small groups of learners with a large bowl of water and several items which would either sink or float.

"No-one touch the water," Tessa voiced sternly, eyeballing each individual.

56

"Hamad, are you going to touch the water?"

"Nooooo Miss."

"Mohammed, are you going to put in your hand," she asked, demonstrating how a hand could go towards the bowl and potentially get wet.

"Nooooo Miss."

"Year 1 Green, are you going to touch the water?" Tessa reiterated slowly and carefully.

"Nooooo Miss Tessa," chorused the throng of six year olds.

Tessa patrolled the class as she was speaking and had just completed a circuit when there was a splash, followed by squeals and shouts. She turned to witness a boy up to his elbows in the bowl of water, delighting in the wetness and sharing his joy with the other children in his learning group.

There were gasps from the rest of the class and maids were called to bring appropriate clean-up cloths and towels. This brief drama dealt with, Tessa moved bravely on with the lesson.

"What do you think will happen to the shell?" she asked, picking up a shell from possible sinkers or floaters and showing it to her class.

There were some blank faces that stared at the ceiling; some children were elbowing each other, clearly not thinking about whether or not a shell would sink or float; some carried on conversations in Arabic; some were looking at the water in the bowl in front of them.

"Ok everyone, find a shell," said Tessa brightly.

Immediately, on that command, the children standing in groups around the carefully set-up experiment tables grabbed whatever came to hand and chucked it into the closest bowl of water.

"Let me count the ways they can fuck things up," Tessa said later over a glass of wine, as she lay on the debriefing couch.

It wasn't just the practical lessons that offered comedic potential. I quite often chuckled out loud as I marked homework. As part of literacy homework, the children in my year four class wrote sentences each week to help them learn new vocabulary. It is laughably obvious when a nine year old has thought up their own idea or copied directly from the internet. One of my all-time favourites was written to illustrate the word 'breeze'.

She found the sea breeze worked wonders for her libido.

(This example still makes me smile in moments when I need a little humour pick-me-up.)

As part of a block of lessons studying the poems of Dr Seuss, the children were asked to bring in a Dr Seuss poem that they liked from home. Some of the children had brought in a page from *Red Fish, Blue Fish*; some had brought in random poems not written by Dr Seuss; some, of course, had not brought anything at all; and one had found a rude adult version of *Cat in the Hat*, with a very vivid description of impotence.

I calmly questioned the individual on their choice of poem outside the classroom, while the other children were occupied with making *Red Fish, Blue Fish* hats for Writers' Week.

"And your mum was OK with the poem you found?" I asked, eyebrows raised.

"Oh yes Miss. She print for me."

During those early days, I get the idea that the school is not so much a place of education, but a daytime facility or baby-sitting service. The children are dropped off in the morning by the school bus, drivers or maids, and picked up again at the end of the day. I felt more and more that, if I just got through the day without anyone killing or dying, I was doing alright. Teaching became a matter of survival and simplicity, and I found myself repeating, repeating, repeating to try and get a point across. Sometimes the lack of understanding was so, that I had to scrap planned lessons and go right back to basics.

It was news, to my nine year olds, that there are twenty-six letters in the alphabet, made up of five vowels and twenty-one consonants. It was also news that our number system is made up of ten digits and that two and eight will always make ten. It was clear that most of the children in my class weren't interested in learning at all, and saw no value in what I had to say. I was a maid after all – at their service. They were simply at school to play and fight and eat their lunch. They spent their time looking forward to getting home so they could plug themselves into their iPad or Xbox and go to the mall to eat junk-food.

"It is what it is," a wise returning teacher had said to me. "Don't think you are here to change anything."

5

Bureaucratic Nightmare

Accepting employment in a country not your own, comes with a certain amount of paper work. Fortunately for me, I had managed to sidestep most of the form filling insanity endured by some of my less fortunate colleagues. My agent had mentioned in an email something about qualifications being verified at the Kuwaiti embassy in London and something else I don't remember, but then suddenly here was my e-ticket and I was on my way.

On arrival at Kuwait International Airport there is nothing to tell you what to do. I queued up at passport control with others from my flight. It had been a long, long time since leaving London the day before. Departure was delayed three hours, so I had missed my onward connection from Abu Dhabi to Kuwait. I had a six hour wait, which would have been very uncomfortable had I not been treated to a few hours of luxury in the Etihad members lounge. An early morning flight completed the journey and I now, in my sleep deprived trance, tried to understand what the immigration officer was trying to tell me.

"Go up," he said, pointing to the stairs.

"Up. OK," I replied.

At the top of the stairs was a café, a bank teller window, some cash machines, and next to that, some rows of seating and some uniformed officials. Red LED lights showed a queuing number system and a noise buzzed to indicate the queue had progress to the next number. Some exhausted looking passengers held pieces of paper with numbers printed on and occasionally looked up to check they hadn't missed their go. Other passengers were bent over filling in forms and copying details from their passports.

After a moment of nutting out the process in my tired old brain, I found the stack of forms to fill in. A kind fellow passenger showed me the button to press to get a number and where the photocopier was to copy my passport.

During this orientation, a uniformed official relaxed at his desk in a corner, scrolling through his phone occasionally nodding and smiling to himself. The officials behind the counter dealt with each passenger, inputting data, stapling and stamping, with the unhurriedness of government officials worldwide. The buzzer sounded, my number appeared and I was issued with a three month visit visa.

Welcome to the State of Kuwait.

Rupert had not been so fortunate in side-stepping bureaucracy. He had diligently followed the directives of his agent and jumped through all the costly immigration and employment hoops, necessary to accepting his position of Head of Primary. He had made the trip to the Kuwaiti embassy in London, from his home in Sheffield, to present his qualification certificates and get a stamp of verification from the officials there. Then, when he arrived, he discovered that he could have entered on a visit visa, as I had done. In fact, because he had left the U.K. before his residency or civil I.D., as it is known, had been finalised, he had to start the application again, from the beginning in Kuwait. This meant he had to pay out again, for all of the paperwork admin and full medical examination.

He was not happy.

Application for civil I.D. takes time; as well as all the medical requirements, there are a lot of trips to the Ministry of the Interior. It also meant that Rupert could not leave Kuwait until the process was complete, otherwise the whole palaver would start from scratch – again!

The civil I.D. circus didn't stop at school. During the year, I met a couple, Brad from Texas, U.S. and Tabitha from Hertfordshire, England. He was an engineer working on some expansion project for Kuwait Oil and she was a teacher at one of the rare 'real' schools up town in Salmiya.

They had met at the Hilton leisure club and had recently got married. They sit side by side on a couch, tanned and middle-age fit from gym work outs and tennis.

"Well, you see, civil I.D. is non-transferable," Brad explained. "I've been here for around ten years as a resident, and because I've changed jobs to a different department, I have to apply all over again. Same company, you understand, just a different department."

Tabitha was working on a spousal visa, which had been cancelled because Brad was in the process of applying for a new civil I.D., so neither of them could leave the country until the application was processed.

"We don't know how long it'll take," she said. "You get passed around from one office to another, then when you find where you're supposed to be, the person who can do what you need doing is on a 'lunch' break, or something. It's really inconvenient and time-consuming."

Three months after we had arrived in Kuwait, and after the rest of us had enjoy two separate holidays and the chance to go travelling somewhere, Rupert finally received his civil I.D. He was legally allowed to work in Kuwait, open a bank account, buy a sim card, receive free medical care and hire a car. The cost of all Rupert's immigration paper work was mysteriously taken from his pay without explanation or warning.

He was not happy.

Apparently, my application for civil I.D. was in the pipe line although, by the time I left Kuwait for the last time, I was still coming into the country on a recurring three month visit visa. No-one from immigration, at the airport, seemed to mind or question me about what exactly I was finding to do as a tourist, for three months at a time. I was always issued a visa and sent on my way.

Missing pay was a common occurrence. One month, I checked my account balance to find I was paid short by two and a half Kuwaiti

Dinar, approximately five pounds. I was both annoyed and curious. It wasn't a huge amount, but there was no explanation for its disappearance. It just seemed as if I had been penalised for some misdemeanor.

"It's just your turn," said Tanya, one of the long-standing teachers from year six. "They do it all the time. Next month it'll be someone else."

There were quite a few teachers who had also experienced the mystery of the disappearing pay. One teacher from Early Years was missing half a month's salary and didn't know why.

"All your questions and queries will be seen to this afternoon at 2p.m., when Mr Fahad from H.R. will be in school," said Cliff at morning briefing. "Please remember, he is just doing his job. He doesn't make the rules. So bare this in mind when you see him and I'm sure he will be able to explain any pay issues you may have."

Sensing the avalanche of disgruntled staff that would descend on reception at two, I decided to forgo classroom prep for the following day, in favour of being first in the queue to see Mister H.R. Fixit Fahad and find out about my missing KD. I settled into the dark brown mock-leather sofa at ten to two and watched the comings and goings of the reception area.

The entrance to school is up some marble steps, through a sliding clear-glass door. Once inside, there are chairs, sofas and coffee tables and a flat-screen TV mounted on the wall. Directly in front of the sliding door is the reception desk, with at least three women busily checking their phones at any one time. To the right is the principal's office and to the left is the school manager, Ms Huda's office, next door to the finance office. It's perfectly clear that the real running of the school happens in the Arabic, left-hand side of the reception desk. The principal's office with its white, English speaking school principal is clearly just for show, like the flat-screen TV.

A few minutes pass, and I am joined by two more teachers. At a little after two, three more arrive and simultaneously, we all look at the clock.

"He's not here yet then," one of them observed.

We all sat, not saying much like patients in a doctor's waiting room. Time ticked away. More teachers arrived. Then Cliff appeared from the principal's office.

"Oh, ummm, he's not here yet then," he noticed, glancing at the clock before disappearing into Huda's office.

A moment later, he appeared again and announced that Mr Fahad was not answering his phone and had left the office and couldn't be found and was probably not coming to the school that afternoon after all. There was a collective sigh and a moan from the congregated staff as, one by one we went back to what we should have been doing in our classrooms, instead of watching the clock in reception.

Having civil I.D. seemed a bit pointless. As a visitor to Kuwait I was working here, although not legally, but I had a bank account organised by the school, and with the help of someone else's civil I.D., was able to buy a sim card. I had no interest in driving, so I wouldn't be hiring a car. The traffic is a nightmare, plus there is nowhere to go. When it came to doctors and hospitals, I absolutely did not want to be at the mercy of the national healthcare. I was happy to learn that some teachers at school had successfully avoided the civil I.D. issue for a number of years and were still coming and going on a three month visit visa, like a revolving door.

Because I was a visitor, with civil I.D. pending, the school was obliged to pay for an exit, before the three months visit visa expired. H.R. needed a copy of the visa and the passport and they would book one night in Bahrain, the cheapest place to fly to from Kuwait. I was not at all happy about going to Bahrain. After browsing pages of the internet, I decided it looked like a dump: something like Kuwait, but with booze. I voiced this one day to Kris, a long-serving staff member from New Zealand.

"You don't have to go to Bahrain. You can book your own trip anywhere and get a cash reimbursement, instead," she said.

This was hugely appealing and I wasted no time in booking a week in Greece for the up and coming half-term holiday. I scanned my visit visa from August, and put in my application for a reimbursement of travel costs to the value of a return flight to Bahrain. This was all good in theory, although I was still waiting for the reimbursement two months later.

The three month visit visa was handy and as a British citizen the minimal fee was waived, but it was not available for all nationalities.

South Africans had to enter the country on a commercial visa. This was more expensive and meant that, until the civil I.D. was processed, my South African colleagues had to leave every month. Not only that, but they had to leave and re-enter Kuwait during a work day and not at the weekend.

The reality of this was that every one out of four weeks, a majority of the primary staff were not in school. They jetted off to Istanbul, as Turkey was one of the few countries open to South African passport holders, and the remaining teachers had to cover their absences in the classroom. On top of this, some genius in H.R. decided, instead of staggering the travel so that only two or three teachers were away at one time, the full herd of South African teachers were out *en masse* every fourth week of the month.

There was whinging all round. The staff that were put 'on cover' complained that they lost their free lesson time for planning and marking. And it seemed to be the same teachers each month that were asked to cover the absent South Africans. There were groans and sighs as we trooped past the staff notice board on the way to flag ceremony each morning, hoping against hope that we would not see our names on the cover roster.

The South African staff complained because the ping-pong effect of air travel was grinding them down. They were often booked on the cheapest flights available, departing and arriving at night and the wee small hours of the morning. Sometimes, they had to leave school early and with just a couple of hour's notice to get to the airport. Also, if their flight arrived before or during school, they were obliged to come in to teach or lose a day's pay, even if they had missed a night's sleep.

"I don't know why they're whining," said Dave one day. "They get an all expenses paid trip to Istanbul every month, while we're stuck here!"

It was the only time that I thought that travelling on a South African passport might be enviable, but you could see their point.

Teachers generally have a reputation for complaining - the school, the kids, the marking, the exams, the reports, the parents, blah, blah, blah. I tend not to whinge, but focus on the holidays and the monthly paycheck, which was why, after all, I took this job. The trick I learned was to keep your head down, do your job and not look for logic in anything, anywhere at any time.

There is a certain amount of admin you expect to do as a teacher: reports midway and at the end of the year; reading records and homework monitoring; data-gathering and grading to chart a child's progress. This grading and charting began with a baseline assessment close to the start of the first term, where the children were given literacy and numeracy tasks to complete to gauge their academic level. My class was a mixed bag. I had a couple of kids who were very able students with excellent English skills at the top, through to the bottom of the bottom, where there were children who could barely write their names. I marked the papers and graded each child accordingly, entering the data on a spreadsheet on the school shared drive. Job done. Or so I thought.

A few days later, my year group were called together for a meeting.

"We have to change the grades," said Olga, our year leader.

There was a directive from management expressing concern that in year four some of the children were input as W.T. or 'working towards'. (Just a note here, that children are graded according to a set of measurable skills which is handily set out on a matrix. By year four, a child is expected to write clearly, use connectives, and generally start to express their ideas clearly in sentences for literacy and to know about number progressions, simple operations and calculations in numeracy. If on an assessment, nothing on the matrix can be ticked off, the child is classified as 'working towards' because they are not at a gradable level yet.) In year four it was assumed that all children would be at least on the first step of the progression ladder.

"But, when a kid can barely write their name and hasn't written anything at all for a writing test, well that is a sure indication of 'working towards'," said Frances, trying to make sense of it all.

"I know," said Olga, "it just doesn't look good on paper, so we have to change it."

"Fine," I said, sticking to my mantra – *Do not look for logic.*

The real reason for 'looking good on paper' was that the school was applying to be accepted as a British School of the Middle East (BSME) and to be endorsed by Council of British International Schools (COBIS). To be part of these organisations showed a legitimacy and a quality education according to British standards, which are regarded internationally as 'high', enabling the school to up their profile and increase their fees.

"There's no way this school's going to be up to scratch," said Tessa, when I told her about fiddling the test levels. "They're dreaming, if they think a few lesson plans and some colourful spreadsheets of grades are going to make a difference. They'll see for themselves on the first inspection visit that this school is utter crap!" She finished this outburst with a snort of derision.

The strange and surprising outcome was that, the school must have met the criteria of both organisations, because the logos of both BSME and COBIS began to appear on all communication material. That, or a lot of money must have changed hands.

The real fun and games, regarding paper work, was saved until the final week of the year, before we all flew away in our separate directions. The children had all started their summer holidays and the teachers were at school tying up loose ends and waiting for the last day. There was no information provided by the school regarding the winding-up procedure. Teachers came to school clocked in then milled about until clocking out time. Once again it was the people who had civil I.D. who were hardest hit, as the civil I.D. needed to be cancelled before leaving Kuwait. Like the application, the cancellation process involved filling out numerous forms and trips to various government departments in a whirlwind, where nothing was straight forward or explained. Teachers were herded around, things were said in Arabic

71

and passports were collected and taken away for a few days. Then, some papers were signed to say that final pay check had been received, when actually it hadn't. Apparently standard procedure.

"Don't worry," said Mr Fahad of H.R., "tomorrow you will get a check – maybe the next day. But first you will sign, then we go to the ministry, they say 'are you happy', you say 'yes', then they take your civil I.D. make hole, then they give back passport. Hallas. Finish."

Once again, there was that feeling that no-one was actually steering the ship. We, the immigrant teachers, were dependent on our masters to follow through with the terms of employment, trusting that they planned to pay up as expected. We were being tossed about on the sea of ignorance, clinging on to a life raft of hope. There was little point in being anxious, but it was hard not to be, and for someone like me who liked to know what was going on, in charge of my own destiny, I was far from comfortable being kept in the dark and fed snippets of information.

As a visitor, still on a three month tourist visa, I once again side-stepped the admin circus of the civil I.D., but that meant I was not eligible to apply for a police check, in preparation for my next teaching post. Dave, however, was on the ball and had made inquiries and searched the internet for information, well in advance of End-of-Days.

The central police station was a taxi-ride away up town in Kuwait City. Dave was dropped off and went in through the main entrance, where there was a lively reception counter crowded with men in dishdashas, holding guns. They were all enthusiastically comparing each other's hardware: police officers nodding and smiling approval, then handing out pieces of paper that turned out to be gun licenses. After looking around for some signage in English, and finding none, Dave fought his way through to a friendly police receptionist, who was busy approving a large shot gun.

Dave held up his passport and civil I.D. and said the words *police check*, hoping to be understood. The friendly policeman indicated that Dave was in the wrong place and that he needed to go outside and round the back. He then pointed with the gun he was holding.

Outside and round the back, there were two doors side by side: one had a sign in English; the other, a sign in Arabic. Dave went through the door of the English signage only to be told he needed to be next door.

The office next door was barely the size of a walk in wardrobe. It was dingy, dirty and dim and manned by a sixteen year old boy, who had just left school. He spoke a little English. Dave duly explained what he required and the boy took down his details and filled out a form. Then he took Dave's passport and said everything would be ready in about a week. At this point, Dave had serious reservations about leaving his passport with a child, in a dirty cupboard, so close to his day of departure, but what choices did he have?

The following week, only days before flying out, Dave repeated his journey up town to retrieve his passport and police check. The same youthful police officer was in charge and recognised Dave from his previous visit. He pulled an over-stuffed ring-binder onto the desk and started to leaf through, stopping occasionally to compare photos on forms with the person who was standing in front of him.

Dave spotted his form and pointed at the photo of himself.

"It's me. Look," he said smiling and pointing from the photo to his face.

The boy appeared confused, looked up at Dave, then looked again at the photo on the form. "Lah," he said and continued leafing through the files.

Dave, who is an imposing figure, stepped forward at this point and slapped an assertive hand on the page to make himself understood.

"Passport. Now. Shukran."

6

Booze

"And did you hear about that poor man in Saudi Arabia, I think it was, who was found with some bottles of something alcoholic, and has been sentenced to three hundred and something lashes?" Mum said in her worried voice.

"Yes, but that's Saudi," I respond to reassure.

Alcohol in Kuwait is illegal, it's true. And I heard all sorts of stories about intoxicated westerners being arrested, imprisoned and deported, but not whipped.

There was the story of a man who had been at a function at the British embassy, who had stumbled out, into a cab and instead of being delivered safely to his address, was taken promptly to a police station. It was rumours like this, that fueled the rumours of why the British embassy did not have bar facilities for expats, anymore.

Human nature generally dictates that when you have no access to something, that something becomes exactly what you really really want. I naturally thought that this would be case for me living with the restricted access to alcohol in Kuwait, where even possession is illegal. This doesn't mean that there isn't any: it's just not readily available.

You can't just pop down to the offie and grab a bottle of pinot gris at the end of a grueling week at the coalface. But to my surprise I wasn't really bothered.

"What? No booze? Nothing? At all? Anywhere?" Steph, a friend from New Zealand, asked over Skype one day. "But surely there are hotels with bars?"

"No."

"What about expat clubs where you have to be a member?"

"Nope. Well maybe at some embassies…."

"But you can get a glass of wine or a beer with a meal in a restaurant?"

"No. Although, you can get a non-alcoholic beverage, which looks like beer."

There was a pause here as Steph processed the information.

"How are you going to cope?"

"I'll be OK. You make me sound like I have a dependency problem. It's not like I'm denying myself anything here - like being the only sober person in a bar on a Friday night. It's not like back home. There's just no drinking culture here."

She wasn't convinced.

"I'll get trashed in the holidays!" I said, finishing on a bright note.

It was my birthday, so I invited the teachers in my building over to my flat for a booze-free birthday bash. I wasn't going to do anything to celebrate. I was happy to let this birthday slide by without public acknowledgement, but then I thought, fuck it. I bought disposable cups, plates and cutlery and blew up some balloons. I put a range of fruit juice in the fridge, loaded up the ice tray, and put peanuts and crisps out in bowls. I played a party mix through my laptop mini-speakers and arranged fairy lights to add a little atmosphere.

Rupert and Sandra were first to arrive.

"Woohoo! Let's get this party started," Rupert said as he boogied through the door.

Tessa from the flat next door came over soon after and we all had a laugh about having a social gathering without booze. The coloured balloons lay idly around the floor.

"It's like being five years old again," Sandra said unwrapping a luxurious chocolate cake. Then she handed me a piece of folded paper, which turned out to be instructions for a microwave. A hand-drawn seagull, wings outstretched over some squiggly waves was on a blank space. Inside was written - *Happy birthday from Rupert and Sandra. Always remember the seagull.* The seagull, gliding above the waves of chaos, skillfully avoiding being sucked down as it dips its wing tips, always serenely souring just above, unaffected. This was the image I held in my head of being a teacher in Kuwait. I was the seagull.

It was just the four of us for ages, then Dave, Simon and Tim arrived fashionably late. I don't know what they were expecting. It's not like there was going to be 'a crowd' or a peak in the evening where everything was going to kick off. No. It was just me with some fairy lights, balloons and my laptop playing a party mix.

"We've just been out for some KFC," said Tim.

"Great," I said. "How was it?"

"Was just like home, except the menu is all in Arabic," Tim replied, sounding surprised.

"When are we going to do the bumps?" said Dave with a big northern grin, chest muscles flexing, barely contained inside a skimpy vest.

A disturbing picture flashed through my mind of my guests holding my arms and legs, then tossing me up into the air to the chant of my age in number sequence.

"......47 (bump) 48 (bump).....49! (bump and drop)."

I quickly wiped this picture from my mind and distracted the musclely, bearded redhead with a balloon. Being a P.E. teacher he immediately took the cue and organised a game. Within minutes, four of us were playing doubles in an extreme game of balloon tennis.

That was our introduction to being booze-free. The end of the working week wind down; the little clink of celebration; the mental full stop and regroup; permission for empty-headed nonsense; time out from being a responsible adult – all booze-free. Life seemed suddenly dull.

But no. This was an opportunity for change, self-discovery, cleansing, a more wholesome existence, a health conscious mindfulness free of the befuddling effects of booze. I would have been fine with this scenario had it not been for some serious peer pressure.

For a weekend soirée at their place, Sandra had tracked down some bootleg date moonshine. It was nasty, thick and strong. I didn't ask where it came from. I simply accepted with grace and gratitude and clinked my glass to the completion of another week. The gathering was the first of many at the neighbours' place. Guests turned up looking elegant and shyly polite. They engaged in quiet conversation, talking about this and that, laughing where appropriate, and generally behaving like grown-ups until the booze kicked in. Then things got messy. Shoes were kicked off, iTunes was turned right up and Rupert played the *Hokey Kokey*, which no-one thought unusual, and everyone joined in. There is no such thing as 'cool' when a bunch of teachers get together and get drunk.

The following day was most definitely The Day After. Tessa didn't surface at all and I was couch-bound and pathetic. It is strange to think that the pivot of social engagement in the western world is alcohol: an evil drug that, if it was introduced today, would never pass the stringent government health and safety criteria in most countries. I hadn't given this much thought until I was living in this place where alcohol consumption was not a thing.

Pretty much in all the places I have visited, people meet, mix and mingle in pubs, bars and clubs where you can get a drink. Almost everyone I know has at least one story of getting shitfaced and falling over, when everything was a blur and the memory is documented in flashes. But you know, it was so much fun and you still made it home OK.

Booze is a strange substance, which of course, affects different people differently. I am an absolute light-weight. After one or two I am having a wonderful time. I am relaxed and happy and I always want to dance. But if I have any more than a couple of drinks, things swiftly turn pear-shaped and there is an extreme mismatch of *what is* and *what is perceived to be*. The night (or day) will invariably roller-coaster out of control and the happy, foolish, drunken me will always go along for the ride because the thinking, rational part of my brain has momentarily shut down. That is when the mayhem of the random is unleashed into the world, fueling tales of memories that cause an inner smirk and/ or shudder.

But the hideous hangover is soon forgotten and it was a full two weeks before Sandra arrived at the door to share a no-fail recipe for home made wine. She and Rupert had weighed up the potential consequences for their illegal actions and thought it would be all worth it.

"We'll just be careful and quiet about it. Who's to know?" she said with a cheeky twinkle in her eye. "A little drinky isn't hurting anyone, now is it?"

Rupert and Sandra had been invited to a friend of friend's apartment: someone they had known in the U.K. These people enjoyed the good life in Kuwait. He was an engineer, or something to do with oil, and she was a lady of leisure who lunched.

"I would be daft to leave now," he said. "The money is just too good. And it's tax-free."

At their flat, Sandra and Rupert were offered a choice of homemade beer; wine - red, white or sparkling; gin or vodka. These people had fine tuned the art of brewing and distilling and were generously more than happy to share their knowledge.

Throwing caution to the wind Sandra and Rupert loaded up their supermarket trolley with the items they needed to start brewing – a 5 litre bottle of water (the container being the important thing here, not the contents), a funnel, four bottles of organic white grape juice with lock and seal tops, and a bag of sugar. They had been given a packet of brewer's yeast - the essential ingredient. The alchemy took around three weeks to turn the sweetness of the juice and sugar into that most wonderful, taken-for-granted, social lubricant.

A small selection of guests were invited to the tasting evening of the first batch. It was delicious and, best of all, potent. Another fun time was had by all. The music was cranked up again and there were a lot of newly invented dance moves. Luckily for me, Sandra and Rupert loved playing host and as we handily lived just across the hall, at the end of a weekend bender, I always got home safely.

The obvious lack of social spaces to let your hair down meant that entertaining at home was what we did to stay sane. But Kuwait was not always the party pooper. On a booze-free flight returning from Greece with Kuwait Air, I got talking to a photographer who occupied the seat next to mine. He had been on a photo-shoot in Bosnia, which he said was beautiful. We talked about the highs and lows of living in Kuwait.

"It's because of the war," he explained. "When Sadam invaded, some religious leaders saw it as a sign that the people had strayed from the true path of Islam. Before that, Kuwait was quite free. Women wore western clothes, you could get a drink. It wasn't, you know, open, but it was tolerated. Not now. People are scared that Allah will turn against them again. That's why it's now very strict. In public. In private, people do what they want."

This made sense, being that booze was banned by the Qur'an and perceived by serious Muslims as wholly unholy. Imbibing in the juice of the grape definitely fits into the Bacchanalian realm of hedonistic enjoyment, rather than sensible, sober Islam. But the double standard of the outward religious intolerance and private anything-goes boozing was more than a bit hypocritical.

Helen, the secondary English teacher, would sometimes report of year ten boys bragging about their boys' trips, with male cousins and uncles, to Dubai where alcohol flowed freely. There was a popular tourist market for Kuwaiti men to sample the pleasures of the flesh that weren't so readily available back home. They had all their sketchy memories immortalized on their mobile phones and were happy to share, especially during an English comprehension lesson.

There was a bit of a do at one of the yacht clubs. It was a fundraiser. The ticket entitled the guest to four vouchers for drinks at the bar. Somehow the yacht club had managed to organise a boozy affair with the supply of home-made liquor, at a public event. A group of secondary teachers had gone along for a laugh.

It was a fairly congenial evening. The teachers in question drank all their four drinks fast and early, so by the time of the fund-raising raffle, they were hammered. One of the items to be raffled was a cheap bottle of whisky. Someone had successfully smuggled this bottle in somehow, possibly by boat, which was admirable.

Delores, my temporary flat mate, had tried to get a bottle of vodka through at the airport. The customs official had confiscated it despite her best efforts and persuasive charm. She was more successful on another occasion, when she had decanted the vodka into shampoo and conditioner bottles. Although she had succeeded in her mission, her after-work vodka tonic would always taste faintly soapy. She didn't really care and knocked it back.

Marjorie was more upfront and cheeky about her smuggling. She correctly thought, "Who is going to suspect a sweet, old grandmother?" and brought a bottle through wrapped in a cardigan and some knitting, in her granny handbag. Cheers to that.

The yacht club raffle of the smuggled bottle of cheap whisky started off sedately enough.

"Who will start the bidding at 20KD?" asked the M.C. on the mic.

No-one in the venue responded to this request or seemed the least bit interested, except a young South African business studies teacher. He was so enthusiastic about owning the bottle of whisky or perhaps the reality of being in a dry country was beginning to sink into his fuzzy, drunken head. Whatever the reason, he stood up and blurted out in a verbal eruption, "ONE HUNDRED KD!"

The company at his table simultaneously laughed and choked in disbelief.

"What were you thinking?" said Ashleigh, a science teacher, in a cold, calm tone.

Clearly, he wasn't thinking because the thinking, rational part of his brain had momentarily shut down.

Encouraged by our neighbours' wine making success, Tessa and I quickly had a rolling supply, with batches labelled with *Boomshanka, Vin de Mangaf*, courtesy of Rupert's artistic talents, at different stages of completion. The danger was, of course, that we would turn into raging alcoholics, so we had to limit our indulgence to end of the week ONLY. End of the week drinks were thus referred to as Drunk Thursday. Often the thought of getting tanked on the sofa at the Ivory Tower was the thing that got me through some weeks.

Although it was fun to party and share a tipple with others, I did enjoy getting plastered on my own. After work on a Drunk Thursday, I'd indulge in a cup of lovely homemade wine and let it gently massage my tired psyche, which had been under attack all week, opening my senses in a big 'AHHH'. Sometimes I would totter up to the roof where the sun had long since hurried over the edge of the horizon, disappearing quickly as though it couldn't wait to leave Kuwait. The sky was now a starry deep indigo above, and the palest cornflower near the earth. I could see the flares of the refinery burn like massive candles in the distance. Street-lights, shop signs and headlamps illuminating street level down below. The hot night breathing the faintest of movement of air and there is a wonderful weightlessness to everything. Then in my tiddly serenity I would descend to my lounge and imagine that I was in some sophisticated dark red velvet club with low light and pulsing beats. I would turn up some funky tunes and dance around the lounge, cup in hand, uninhibited by any onlookers. Oh yes, what a night, giving a whole new meaning to 'house music'. Or maybe that was the meaning of 'house music' and I was just catching up. By around seven-thirty, I was drunk and hungry, and I departed my imaginary club to forage in the fridge, before a bath and bed.

7

Sex

"Sex".

The voice was low and the 'e' sound was long and drawn out.

"Sex".

Once again, said so only I could hear, as I waited for a gap in the traffic, crossing the road.

The man who persisted in saying the word 'sex' stood just far enough away so as not to draw the attention of passersby, but was close enough for me to hear.

"Sex".

He had followed me from the supermarket. I had noticed his presence as I left the comforting air-con and stepped out into the blazing afternoon sun.

It had been a particularly trying day at the coalface. I had broken up a number of fights; and one of the boys in my class had been in such a hurry to get a drink at the end of break-time, that he had skidded on the wet floor and slammed his head against the metal edge of the water cooler, which instantly issued forth a lot of blood from the centrally located wound. After falling to the ground, he bravely stood, only to faint and fall down again. This was all witnessed by me, my class and a buzz of year two children, who had been released onto the quad for their break. Mohammed was then carried/ dragged to the school doctor's office which thankfully was only a few metres away.

Needless to say, the afternoon's learning was infused with worried Arabic voices. The planned science lesson was overruled with continued assurance that Mohammed was going to be fine; that he would not die in the doctor's office; that his personal classroom items did not have to be packed up and taken to his brother's class; that he did not need to be taken anything from his bag. He didn't need anything to eat or drink and most of all, I reiterated, he just needed to be left alone.

Mohammed was bandaged up and sent home.

I had sought solace in food shopping, which as it turned out was not as consoling as I had hoped. The brand of 100% pure orange juice which boasted 'most pulp' was not where it should have been in the chiller. I stared at the emptiness, contemplating a morning without my juicy kick-start before, sighing audibly, I resentfully grabbed an inferior brand, knowing my day was going to be ruined due to a lack of bits in my juice.

This is the level of smallness that my life had been reduced to living in Kuwait. That a minor detail of which orange juice I started my day with, had been blown up out of all proportion and could have a very real damaging affect on my day.

A bit depressed, I shuffled off to the checkout and stood in line.

At first, I didn't pay much attention to the young man in western clothing, wearing glasses, a stripy shirt, sweat pants and a back pack. He stepped aside at the sliding doors, so I could leave before him. I must have uttered some thanks and kept walking, without making eye contact. A plastic shopping bag in each hand and my school bag slung across my shoulder, I trudged through the parked cars and aimed for home.

That is when I noticed that the aforementioned young man was walking in the same direction, a few metres behind. I slowed to let him pass, then changed direction and marched purposefully on through the car park of the Arabic school. Without looking back, I watched him through sunglasses and periphery vision like a spy, as he doubled back after my change of course. I now knew he was definitely following me.

"Right" I thought. "Bring it on."

My hands gripped the shopping bags as if they were weapons and I checked the possible escape routes. Straight ahead was a busy road I had to cross to get to my street. Left was a traffic roundabout and right was a residential area and the old teachers' building – all pretty public, all out in the open. Behind was an empty car park and some dusty hedges – definitely dodgy.

I marched to the street and stood waiting for a break in the traffic so I could cross the road.

"Sex".

This time the hairs on the back of my neck bristled with indignation.

How dare he? I thought, and still I was prepared for him to walk away quietly and leave me alone. The longer we stood there waiting for the traffic to clear, the angrier I became. What did he think would happen? Was I going to turn to him smile sweetly, drop my shopping and my knickers, say 'come on then big boy', and do it then and there on the pavement? Did he really think that I was the tiniest bit interested in having sexual relations with a complete stranger who had followed me from a supermarket? Is that really how he found girlfriends or attracted women? Did he really for one minute think that saying the word sex over and over was going to make it actually happen? Was he totally deluded or perhaps really really arrogant that he assumed he was so unbelievably irresistible that I would jump at the chance to jump him?

I was snorting through flared nostrils, enraged; an animal ready to charge.

"Sex."

That was it. I summoned the spirit of Kali and imagined me as her, multi-armed, a dagger in each hand apart from the hand holding the severed head of the unfortunate man who had dared to approach me. Kali, goddess of destruction, bulging eyes, massive carnivorous teeth, shaking with the anger of every woman who had ever been mistreated, beaten, raped, abused or intimidated rose up inside me. Kali, pounding the bodies of abusers, stamping down the mistreaters until they were bloodied mud under her stomping feet. And with this spirit of nightmares, I took a deep yogic breath and bellowed with the force of hell.

"FUCK OFF!"

The young man seemed at once surprised and embarrassed. He scurried away without turning back. Some pedestrians on the opposite side of the street turned to see what had happened. There was a space between cars. I took my chance and darted across.

On the exact same spot a few months later, I was lightly touched on the bottom by a man as I walked home from school. The playful intimacy of the action made me jump with astonishment and incredulity. As I turned to face my assailant, he slowly backed away. It was as if he had a burning need to touch me to see if I was real; as if he expected me not to be. Then by touching me and finding out I that was real, he had found this truth simply unbelievable. The expression on his face was shock and surprise. His hand was still outstretched from the dastardly deed and there was only the briefest pause for assessment from both parties, before I roared a verbal obscenity and he, who had regained his faculties, had turned and scarpered.

Luckily, for him he was fast on his feet and disappeared behind an apartment building before I could pummel him to a pulp. I was ready to cause actual bodily harm and it is a good thing that he got away. I decided that this particular felon was most probably simple of mind and filed the event under 'amusing story', soon after.

Another time, when I was out walking to the beach, a driver in a utility van slowed to my pace and hissed out of the window "Hey you, fuck me, how much?" I quickly ducked round some roadside skips and walked back the way I had come, head down, not looking, trying to be as invisible as possible. But in that moment, I remember thinking what a clever and efficient use of language: almost haiku in its simplicity.

These incidents were not unusual and didn't scare me. I had become used to the attention of being a blonde western woman in an Arabic country. Cars slowed, men leered and yelled things. Some pretended to be taxis 'where you want to go?' Some sort of attention was expected every time I left the flat. The perception seems to be that, by the sheer nature of being a western woman in the Middle East means, you are permanently up for it.

I was not alone in accumulating stories of unwanted attention. Helen had been followed almost to her door by a school aged lad while she was out for a run one day. He couldn't seem to understand that she had absolutely no interest in him at all, on any level.

Tessa has had to endure the attentions of a man at the Ooredoo shop: Ooredoo being one of Kuwait's mobile and internet providers. She had an issue with her sim card and went back to the shop to try and sort it out. The man was pleasant at first, but then the conversation turned. For the purposes of storytelling I shall call him Ahmed. He is middle aged with a stomach that stretches the limits of his shirt buttons. He has no neck.

Ahmed: It is nice to see you again. I miss you.

Tessa: Yes well, the sim card you sold me doesn't seem to be working.

Ahmed: I think perhaps you like me. Yes?

Tessa: Umm. Could you change it for me?

Ahmed: We can go for shisha sometime. You give me your number.

Tessa: No. And besides it doesn't work.

Ahmed: I give you new sim card and you call me, yes?

Tessa: Um no. I have a husband. (A lie in an attempt to deflect attention.)

Ahmed: And I have wife. I no like. She fat. I like you. I......want.....you.

Tessa eventually received a replacement sim card and left the Ooredoo shop with a hearty laugh, as Ahmed, although repulsive, posed little threat.

This is very much a man's world and for men, getting sex is quite straight forward, as there are a multitude of 'massage parlours' to choose from. A colleague in a different apartment building to ours, often shared the lift with customers on their way to the second floor, for a 'massage', particularly late at night. The linger of their *oud* stayed in the lift long after they had gone.

Filipino pimps regularly patrolled the exits to supermarkets, handing cards to male shoppers for a massage at home or an all-girl cleaning service. Women didn't get approached in this way, because women are part of the service not the recipient of the service.

I accidently walked in on a Filipino sex worker in a public toilet at Al Kout. She had not locked the door of the cubicle and was filming herself posing in lime-green lacy knickers, pouting into the camera for an online client. There are some things I wish I could unsee. Sex, in Kuwait, is something done by a man to a woman, where the woman is there for the pleasure of the man, it seems.

In reference to homosexuality, I don't feel I can comment as I was not made aware of it. There are no Red Light districts or gay bars of course, but my feeling is that the gay community is alive and well although very much underground and behind closed doors. It would not be difficult for men or women to cultivate same sex coupling because of cultural sexual segregation: men spend a lot of time with other men, away from the women and children. Also, the gay community is not publicly acknowledged because of the ultra conservative religious constraints. The teachings of Islam deny the existence of that sort of thing. Homosexuality is viewed as a sinful and perverted deviation from the norm of heterosexuality: sex is for making babies, full-stop.

At school there is no sex ed. Anything to do with reproduction is strictly off-limits. There are not even any labels for the male and female parts of the flower. That's not to say that there isn't teenage sex experimentation. It just happens off-shore at boys' weekends away, to places like Dubai, where all the fun and games are captured for bragging, on iPhones.

To illustrate the lack of sex knowledge, one of Helen's friends who is a nurse in Saudi, interviewed a young, newly married couple when they came to the clinic where she worked. They were a little embarrassed to admit that, although they had been going at it like rabbits, she had not yet conceived. A brief examination revealed the reason: her hymen was still intact.

Some women have cleverly exploited the clear sex divisions and used them to their financial advantage. Marie, an ESOL teacher at the Ministry of Defense, noticed that there was something not quite right about the new English teacher when she arrived for work one morning. Although the woman was dressed as a Muslim, with her head demurely covered with a scarf, her shoes were shiny, white platforms with killer six-inch stiletto heels. She wore a lot of make-up, had bright red nails and beneath her loose outer clothing was a sumptuous body of voluptuous curves that she showed off in a haughty, hip-swinging strut. And there was just a tad too much cleavage.

It turned out that this was no English teacher, but a Puerto Rican porn star. During her brief employment at the MoD, she had persuaded her male boss to advance her a month's salary. She had also extorted thousands of Kuwaiti Dinar from her students and even from an unsuspecting male colleague. No-one had done an adequate background check and the true nature of this femme fatale was not discovered until the day she mysteriously disappeared.

94

By contrast there are, of course, all sorts of horror stories in circulation about women who have been attacked on the street, walking by themselves at the beach or being duped into opening their front door to a stranger, only to be attacked in their own homes.

We were warned at school briefings to be vigilant and to never venture out alone especially at night. This advice was taken lightly by me and my pals, because who can actually live like that? Sex attacks are not exclusive to Kuwait. Unfortunately, people are attacked all over the world and statically Kuwait is one of the safest places to live. But still there is a general feeling of being objectified as a woman, like nowhere else I have travelled.

When I leave the apartment I wear clothing that covers. The standard teaching uniform that I wear for work is universal: modesty is the key; skirts below the knee, tops with a high neck, no revealing items, no unnecessary distracting flesh. And on my non work days, I go out as if on manoeuvres; khaki pants, plain t-shirt, hair stuffed up inside a hat, shades on, and my trusty old go-anywhere Birkenstock sandals. I walk, head down, not looking at anyone, not making eye-contact, just purposefully striding with a 'don't mess with me' attitude.

In this place I do not want to be pretty or seen or noticed by anyone. I am here to do my job and that is all. Singletown is where I live and I'm quite happy here, and being a single gal in Kuwait is easy. There is very little temptation. I live simply, nun-like in the Ivory Tower, oscillating from home to school and back again; sometimes via the supermarket to collect food essentials; sometimes to Al Kout beach to see the water. That is the sum of my existence.

The lack of alcohol means those taken-for-granted places of public mingling such as pubs, bars and clubs are missing here. I had almost forgotten how and where I meet people at all, let alone potential romantic encounters. Sometimes in my puritan life of enforced abstinence, I have thought how nice it would be to have some eye-candy once in a while; some beautiful physical specimen of a man to just fancy from afar, just to know that he exists; someone that you could just summon into your head during a vacant moment or a staff meeting. But in Kuwait, as my dear friend, flat mate and colleague Tessa, pointed out 'There's slim pickings here'. Kuwait is a desert in more ways than one.

I believe this lack of attractive men is partly due to the aesthetic of Middle Eastern traditional dress still worn by a majority of Kuwaitis. The *dishdasha*, an ankle-length white, high necked, long-sleeved robe worn with a *gutra*, a square piece of fabric, which is folded into a triangle and held in place on the head with the *ogal*, a double circlet of twisted black cord – is a look that has not changed in hundreds of years. In this garb, the modern Kuwaiti man bears little resemblance to the charismatic character played by Omar Sharif in *Lawrence of Arabia* and a group of dishdasha clad men possess the same comic appeal of a bunch of lads, in dress-ups on a stag night.

In fact, there are no hot men in Kuwait. Apart from one. Once, and only once in my time here did I notice a sexy man. One.

He was spotted by Tessa and me one Saturday evening. We were quietly idling away the last few hours of our weekend, not doing very much when we noticed the sound of sirens approaching. From our eighth floor window we could clearly see a stream of emergency vehicles – fire engines, ambulances, police cars – speeding from the route 30 exit, past the mosque, to our building.

"Mmmmm is our building on fire?" I asked, opening the apartment door and sticking my head out to listen for drama and smell for smoke. All quiet.

We scampered up onto the roof and saw that the parade of flashing lights and sirens were gathering at a building behind ours, which had smoke billowing from an upper storey window. We watched for a while from the rooftop, then the need for a closer look and sheer entertainment got the better of us and we ventured down to the street.

There was a carnival atmosphere at ground level. Men were congregated in groups, laughing and pointing; families had brought their dinner to eat, picnic style among dusty vehicles and piles of rubbish; children darted about between the onlookers and emergency vehicles, playing chasing games.

Tessa and I took our place and watched as a rescue unfolded. There were three fire engines already in position, next to the burning building (I say 'burning' here as an assumption because there was smoke but we didn't see any flames). Three more fire engines arrived as we stood there, carefully chugging through the crowd.

A crane from one of the fire engines was elevated to a balcony, where two adults and a child waited to be lifted to safety. A cheer went up from the crowd as they were brought down to earth. The crane then went up again, this time to a balcony on a lower floor. There seemed to be some animated discussion as the rescuer arrived and the crane left with only one of the rescuees. The crane did not come down straight away, but rose up again to a higher floor, but did not stop to take on more passengers. It was then lowered, so it's one passenger could get off before rising up again. After watching for a while, there seemed to be no plan to the rescue and the crane appeared to be used as an amusement park ride. There was a distinct lack of urgency that you would expect from a rescue mission from a flaming building.

The street was now packed with onlookers and emergency service vehicles and personnel. The atmosphere had disintegrated from a village fair to reckless rabble. There was shouting and gesticulating, beeping of horns and whirring of sirens. There was a scuffle and some shoving. We decided to move on.

Instead of going back the way we had come, we thought it would be fun to return to our apartment via a route past the burning building, round the block and back up the other side, thus completing a satisfying circuit of the neighbourhood. We were out. Why not make a night of it?

The flashing lights pulsed disco colours up the blank apartment block walls and as we passed the main entrance to the burning building, there he was.

"Pinch me. I'm dreaming," said Tessa.

"Oh my lord, he's gorgeous," I mumbled without daring to move.

The night felt suddenly silent and the world slowed to a breathless stop. Only the coloured lights kept up their heartbeat display.

We were standing on the road between the fire engine and the steps leading up to the building and he, like a male-stripper was on the stage of the entrance, illuminated by the flashing fire engine lights and his own absolute beauty.

He had obviously just come down from some heroics in the burning building. He had pulled his blue standard issue boiler suit off his shoulders, revealing a trim muscular torso in a white vest daubed with smudges of soot. His skin shone with a sweat of someone who had exerted his well-toned body doing something selfless and worthy. He held a plastic water bottle up to his lips and tilted it to take a long, deep, quenching slug. Then (and this is my favourite part), he closed his eyes, raised the bottle above his head allowing the water to stream down his face, causing rivulets down his neck to his perfect chest and making wetness across his stomach and into his partially undone overalls.

My, oh my. What a treat!

Did we stand there mouths agape like a couple of goldfish? We did. Did we potentially obstruct professional emergency service personnel in their line of duty with blatant gawping, and mindlessly placed ourselves between a burning building and a fully operative fire engine? This is true. Did we, without any shadow of a doubt, sexually objectify a man in a public space, who was trying to do his job? Guilty as charged.

The spell was broken all too soon by an irate man who was trying to drive his SUV through a gap between the fire engine and a parked car that was clearly too narrow. Judging from the gasps and oooohs from the watching crowd, it was obvious to everyone except the man driving, that there was no way the SUV would fit. It didn't. The driver became enraged by his own stupidity and the attention of the watching crowd as he dented and scratched the paint off his car, the parked car and the fire engine.

The unmistakable sounds of crunching and scraping of metal against metal attracted even more attention from the rubber-neckers who had become bored by the lack of drama of the fire incident. The sexy fire fighter was lost to us as a crowd gathered to view the damage and we drifted, as if in a dream, round the block and back to our apartment.

Tessa and I would often remember that night and reminisce about the way the hot fireman had put on a show just for us. Was he really as gorgeous as we remembered? Or has the drought of sexy men in Kuwait skewed our perception and made an average bloke seem more gorgeous than he actually is? Either way, the event has become legendary at the Ivory Tower, going some way to restore the gender balance of sexual objectification, and was a welcome relief to two single ladies who hadn't seen a sexy man in a long, long time.

8

Violence

"I get it now," hissed Frances close to my ear at flag ceremony, one morning.

"What do you get?" I hissed back, like a ventriloquist, trying not to move my mouth.

"The violence," she replied.

A child had just finished a reading from the Qur'an. The translation into English was this...

> *If you think something is improper, try to change it with your hands.*
> *If you cannot, then try to change it with your words.*
> *If you cannot, then consider it improper inside yourself.*

Flag ceremony was morning assembly when the whole school lined up in class order to sing the national anthem, hear a reading from the Qur'an and an inspiring few words from the principal, as well as receive notices of current events. I had not paid much attention to the content of flag ceremony, most of it being delivered in Arabic through a P.A. system that sometimes worked. My mind tended to drift away to my happy place; a sun lounger on a beach in Goa, a margarita served on a tray, the sun lazily sinking down to meet the sea at the horizon.

Now that Frances had pointed out the words in the reading, the thinking did appear to be upside down. Surely you don't attempt to change the world by force before negotiating first, and then if you can't make any changes you just keep quiet? It did seem a bit odd. And then there were the lyrics from the national anthem. Each teacher was given an English translation to learn and file.

Kuwait, My Country, May you be safe and glorious!
May you always enjoy good fortune!
You are the cradle of my ancestors, who have distinguished themselves in this world, and immortalized themselves with their heroic deeds and martyrdom, and are to be found like stars shining in Paradise.

Kuwait, land of heroic martyrs: a place where dying while defending country and beliefs was celebrated every day through children singing at school assemblies. These examples of accepted violent imagery went some way to explain the children's unacceptable classroom behaviour and societal norms into which they were born.

On a more positive note, flag ceremony always finished up with, *Thank you for your attention. I wish you the best.*

I had borrowed a book from a colleague entitled *The Arabs: a History* by Eugene Rogan, to learn more about the culture of Kuwait and the Arab people in general. It was weighty in detail and a harrowing read. At every page turn there was conflict and inter-tribal fighting to lay claim to land, wealth and power. The pattern seemed to be, that a tribal leader gets together with some like-minded folk, and convinces the people in the neighbouring areas that he would look after them and make sure that they were protected and that justice would be served. In return, the men would volunteer their services as soldiers and either vanquish their oppressors or go on a jihadist rampage to convince the wider population that their leader should be the leader for everyone. Then one of two things happens: the leader achieves his objective builds a big palace/ fortress, or takes over an existing one, gives all his mates the cushy jobs as magistrates and tax-collectors; or he fails in his objective, the oppressors take back control in a nasty bloodbath, as a warning to any other would-be contenders.

It is a big fat book, masterfully written and full of facts. I read it on weekend afternoons on my couch at the Ivory Tower, quite often having to pause and take a breather before continuing on to read a further chapter packed with conflict and death. Reading this book was far from a relaxing past-time and I always felt a little battered by what I had read.

As I paused for a moment between bouts of bloodshed, the muezzin would summon the faithful to prayer at the mosque only metres from my head. Sometimes this was an engaging sound of someone truly blessed with a singing voice. Often, it was not and the wailing grated and had to be endured. Cars pulled up, men hurried across the vacant lot to roll out their prayer mats and listen to the Islamic thought of the day.

Sometimes the words amplified through a loud speaker system seemed friendly and wise. Often, they seemed angry and tyrannical. I imagined what was being said to the religious assembly...

Go to the building across the street and kill the white teachers!

They are the infidels. They are the non-believers and the enemies of Allah, the great and powerful.

You must show you are worthy of being Allah's chosen people by finding the teachers, especially the ones living on the top floor who cover their ears to block out the sound of my prayers.

I know for a fact they make filthy wine and get drunk after work on a Thursday.

They have even objectified our brave fire-fighters with lustful thoughts.

They must die! They must die! They must die!

Most probably this is nowhere near what was actually said, but the mind plays tricks, especially with reports of ISIS and that Jihad John, the executioner, was originally from Kuwait.

"You're as mad as a bag of spiders, so you are," Tessa's friend from Galway told her before she left. "I wouldn't go to that place for any amount of money. It's the desert you know. No water an' you'll see camels 'n' all will ya?" In small town Ireland the close knit community tends to look inwards and not out. On visits home to visit her family, Tessa would be asked what it is like in 'Emericar', the name describing anywhere that isn't Ireland. People she ran into on the street seemed genuinely surprised that she was still alive and intact.

I suppose that maybe we did seem a bit mad, because if you look at a map, it does appear that Kuwait is right up close to all the unrest in Syria and Iraq, but here in Mangaf, a ghetto of migrant workers, it feels like a place no-one knows or cares about. I feel that we are living on the edge of the earth and that life is happening somewhere else. It was strange to feel like that in Kuwait, after living in New Zealand, which really is far, far away.

Anyway, *scary* or *mean world syndrome* is a very real thing to some people who consume a lot of media, especially television. The potent imagery of violence presented by the media creates anxiety and fear that is out of proportion with reality. Any place outside their immediate boundary is perceived as harsh, hostile and dangerous. No wonder really, considering the continuous bombardment of negative imagery of the Middle East, to the comfortable living rooms of western households, where family and friends watch, expecting the worst.

The Arab world is undoubtedly harsh, which stems from a physical environment of extremes: mostly desert, unbearably hot and dry during the summer months and freezing at night during winter. Natural resources of water and productive land are scarce, so historically people have had to fight hard to defend their territorial rights to available resources.

The Ottoman Empire took a big chunk of time and land mass from the Arabs: based in Turkey and stretching across North Africa to Morocco and East to the Arab Peninsula. Like any empire the cost of keeping the various and many subjects subdued eventually outweighed the income and benefits, so the Ottomans eventually, with the First World War as catalyst, lost control and pulled out of Arabia. The fall of the Ottomans caused a massive power vacuum that was filled with a succession of power-hungry despots, all keen for the easy life of the rich and powerful, with the teachings of Islam at the core of their ideology.

With some understanding of the history of the region, it seemed to me that the children in school still had this idea that fighting is the only way to solve issues, and that you are either the oppressor or the oppressed. So far in my classroom, most of my energy and effort had been spent on 'putting out fires' i.e. breaking up low level disturbances and confrontations. It was exhausting. Every day I sent boys for time-out in Frances' classroom next door, or Rupert's office, to isolate them from other children, in the hope that the rest of the class could get some learning done.

I was comforted to learn that it wasn't only my class that was presenting this kind of behaviour. The whole school was a seething cauldron of violence. "He said bad word for my mother," was commonly heard across all year groups in primary and secondary, and "He do for me like this," which was accompanied by a demonstration of hitting or kicking, was also usual.

Even in Tessa's year one class there were six year olds who displayed some quite disturbing violence. One boy regularly pinched, hit and kicked other children in class, and although he had minimal English, he knew how to say "I will slit your mother's throat and put fireworks in your mouth."

And it wasn't only the children that demonstrated violent tendencies. Rupert was horrified with the way some parents treated their children. The worst incident was when he witnessed a father punching his son in his office, after he had called the parent in to talk about the child's behaviour at school. One mother told me that she was absolutely fine with me hitting her child, if I needed to. It was clear that violence was a vicious cycle that had been passed down the generations and showed no sign of stopping.

The violence in school was the deciding factor which finally tipped the balance to make Simon 'jump'. He took the job in Rome and bragged about how well equipped his classroom was and how much money he was making and how he didn't have to break up fights anymore. But he missed us all. Especially Dave. We were relieved he had gone. Especially Dave, who relished having the flat to himself for a while. He spread his things around, bought an *Xbox* and didn't do the dishes for days on end. He loved living alone in his lad pad.

Simon's position of head of science was filled in a couple of weeks with a science teacher from the States who had just finished a contract in the Dominican Republic.

"It was nice," he said. "Weed was cheap, but the school fucked me over and didn't pay out my final month, so I had to take the first offer, which was here. I don't know how long I'll be staying. There aren't even any Bunsen burners!"

He was also called Simon, but insisted on being addressed as 'doctor', which got everyone's backs up. He did not last long as he just could not handle the kids. From day one you could tell he riled them. The final straw came when he confronted a large year ten boy, who became enraged and ripped a tap from one of the sinks in the science lab. He then chased the unfortunate teacher, who had a limp from a motorbike accident, with the broken piece of plumbing while shouting Arabic obscenities.

I was on a break and heard the ruckus from the marking room. Eager for a glimpse of drama, I poked my head round the corner to see Sandra, who is a very little person, holding back a tidal wave of crazed, testosterone pumped teenage boys, while Simon, eyes wide with glasses crooked on his face, scarpered as best he could with a gammy leg, and shut himself in Rupert's office.

Management decided to address the violence issue by introducing a school anti-bullying week. Each year group were to prepare an assembly and devote some lesson time to talking about bullying –what it is and how to stop it.

I had volunteered my class to lead the year four anti-bullying week assembly. The children were excited by the prospect of performing and enthusiastically acted out scenarios of violent bullying. We devised a short piece of three examples of conflict that the children had come up with. Each one was played out twice. The first time round there would be some sort of bullying. The second time round the children presented a non-violent alternative or a solution to the conflict.

I was really impressed by the way my class was totally committed to their performance. We practiced in the classroom, tables pushed back to the walls and then on stage downstairs in the theatre. Only five boys were not allowed to participate because they could not stop hitting each other. They watched from the side spaced widely apart.

The children glowed with pride when they received rapturous applause from the other year four classes and commendations from the teachers. You could tell they were so happy to have done a great job.

All was well until we walked back to class.

Most of the class had made it back to the classroom as quietly and orderly as could be expected, and I was about to step through the door when a shout went up.

"Fight, fight, Ahmed and Mohammad, they fight!"

I quickly backtracked and rounded the corner to see a pair of glasses punched from a boy's face. The two boys in question were now rolling round the floor in full combat. A teacher from a classroom close by had come to lend assistance and we each grabbed one of the assailants.

Parents were called. Statements were written. Both boys were suspended for three days.

Meanwhile, in the secondary department up on the third floor, there had been a fracas between an I.C.T. teacher and a year nine boy. Other teachers bravely stepped into the fray to calm the, by now, ballistic teacher who was throwing punches left and right, indiscriminately at all persons in his way. He was heard to be screaming "Those fuckin' kids!" and "You bastards!" and "I'll get you!" The teacher had clearly lost it and was instantly dismissed never to be seen again.

I'm not sure how successful anti-bullying week had been. There seemed to be a general increase in crazy like never before. It was as if anti-bullying week just gave the kids more scope and ideas for violent behaviour, rather than stem the flow.

There was an emergency staff meeting after school one afternoon.

"We have received a message from the British embassy today urging people to be on 'high alert' regarding possible terror attacks," said Rupert holding a print out he was reading from.

He continued, "ISIS have warned that they are targeting immigrants, specifically teachers, in the following countries: Egypt, Saudi Arabia, U.A.E, Qatar and Kuwait. Now, I don't know what this means, but we should all be vigilant, keep your phones handy at all times, don't go out on your own, especially at night, you know, um, be careful, I suppose. We'll wait to hear more, but if anyone wants to leave now, that is completely understandable and no-one will have a problem with it."

There were murmurs and low voices of concern.

For the first time in my life I felt victimized. Hearing that a terrorist organisation was singling out foreign teachers to potentially harm, was suddenly like having a target stamped on my head. Here in Kuwait, teachers were so obvious. Our clockwork trail to school and back was easy to track and we looked western in every way.

Possibly, the only way I could blend in would be to wear a niqab and abaya. However, the floor length national dress for women had its own dangers. I once witnessed a woman get stuck on an escalator at the supermarket. I remember thinking how easy it would be for the fabric of the abaya to get caught by the teeth, as the steps disappear at the top, where you get off. And that is exactly what happened, at the exact time I had that thought. The woman was OK, and fell down within easy reach of the emergency stop button.

It also worried me to see women driving wearing the niqab, which covers most of the face only allowing for the eyes to be seen. When you are behind the wheel in any traffic, but especially here where road rules are lax, you don't really want any visual impairment. Another reason I didn't want to drive.

Anyway, I was not going to wear an abaya. Helen, the secondary English teacher had one, and wore it when she worked in Saudi. She loved it. She could go out in her pyjamas: abaya over the top. Who's to know? It was her protection. She even wore it when she went jogging.

Back at the Ivory Tower, Tessa and I mulled over our options regarding the ISIS threat.

"What does this mean – 'be vigilant'?" she said. "Are we going to walk around looking at everyone in the street as if they are potential attackers, bombers, rapists, kidnappers? Nooooooo."

"I can't live my life like that. In fear. And besides," I continued, "this is Kuwait and not only is Kuwait a low profile target, compared to Egypt, let's say; we are in Mangaf. Let's not forget that. If terrorists want to make a statement targeting expat teachers, they're surely going to hit Salmiya before this little out-of-the-way ghetto."

That said, I did experience some incidents of random violence where some youths in dishdashas shouted 'American' at me in the car park outside the Sultan's Centre. They threw glass bottles at my feet. I wasn't really paying attention because they had yelled out 'American', but I was a bit shocked by the shattering glass on the tarmac. I hurried inside the supermarket and hoped they would go away by the time I came out. Luckily they did, not that I was intimidated by these boys. I had built up a hard and angry exterior in defense of endless unwanted attention in the street, and I was quite used to physically breaking up fights. Violence was getting to me. The longer I stayed; the more it seemed normal.

We were advised not to travel by public bus. I had little cause to travel anywhere as there was nowhere to go, other than the beach or a mall, so I really didn't leave my immediate area. But early on, in that first week's holiday, I did catch an uptown bus to have a look around.

I tend to travel by bus wherever I am. It may not be quick, but you get to see real people going about their real lives, so much more than you would if you took a taxi.

I get to the downtown area and decide that there is really not much happening. A trip to uptown Kuwait City is really not worth the bus fare, but at least I made the effort. I have a brief look around and find the bus for the return trip home. I find a window seat in the front row of the raised section at the back of the bus. It's a good place to see everything. The bus stops and I am joined by a friendly American. We start chatting.

"You're brave," he says.

"I am?" I reply.

"The ladies' seats are down front."

Mark is forty years old and a retired marine. He tells me he is making a packet doing his old job, jet plane maintenance, for the Kuwait military. He has a huge Cheshire cat grin as he tells me all about it. He is taking the bus for the same reason as me - just to have a look around.

The bus is full of passengers now. All the seats are taken and people are standing in the aisle, talking on phones, hanging on to the hand straps, trying not to lose their balance. It is hot.

The bus stops. There's no room for anymore passengers and the driver shouts something at a man trying to get on. The driver tries to close the door and drive away, but the man has a foot on the step and he launches himself at the driver, shouting loudly. The driver stops the bus and retaliates. Now it's really hard to know what is going on. Other passengers have joined in and everyone with an opinion is shouting it out. Down at the front of the bus there's a blur of waving arms and aggressive words. Pretty soon, the problematic passenger is hauled off the bus by some of the passengers. The driver regains his composure, straightens his skull cap and we continue on our way, incident-free.

Buses, I learned, were also targets for race hatred. Because low-paid immigrants tend to take the bus rather than more expensive taxis, bored youths were known to hail a bus, as if they were passengers, only to pelt the windows with rocks, to intimidate the people inside. This happened to the bus I was travelling on one day. You could see groups of young men, waiting for the bus to slow down, before hurling their missiles, aiming first at the windscreen and then at the passenger windows. One rock hit the windscreen causing a chip and a crack, and another smashed through one of the windows down the back of the bus. There were yells and screams as the driver pulled over and he, and the inspector, jumped out and gave chase to the attackers. Fortunately, for me, it was my stop and I quickly walked away wishing myself invisible and thanking my lucky stars.

Despite living in what seemed like a terrorist hot-spot, we were probably safer here than in any European capital. I grew up in London, which was notorious for terror threats, and sadly Islamic extremists had already made a statement with violence there in the tragic attack of 5 July 2005.

We kept a close eye on international news developments, waiting for what was going to happen next. Would the threat of violence against foreign teachers be played out? Or would it just slide by and be forgotten? We waited and went about our daily business of teaching children.

After the winter break, a new boy joined my class. He was one of those high energy kids with no off switch. He was happy enough in a manic unsettling way. I introduced him to the class and said things to aid the transition of acceptance. To help with the group dynamic and as part of a literacy component, I tried to get the children to think about their likes and dislikes. They had a few minutes to think of three of their favourite things and three of their least favourite things, and form sentences that expressed their ideas. I gave examples…

"I <u>like</u> chocolate," I said brightly. "I <u>don't like</u> people calling out when I am speaking," I followed up as the noise level erupted with the word 'chocolate'.

I chose a few children who I knew would have some idea about what was required.

"I like playing on my iPad," said one girl. "I don't like my brother."

"I like going to Kidzania," said a boy. "I don't like maths."

I encouraged the children and more hands went up, eager to share.

"Ahmed," I chose the new boy who was about to launch into space with enthusiasm.

"I like guns and money and war," he gushed.

There was a moment's silence while I tried to decide how to deal with this information. Then, I simply acknowledged his input and moved on to the next participant.

As well as this new kid, there was another future terrorist in my class, who managed to create weaponry from anything he could get his hands on. Mohammed was subversive and clever with his terrorism. I noticed that the backs of a couple of chairs in my class were starting to wobble. On closer inspection, it seemed as if the screws were coming out. Then it became apparent that this boy was removing the screws and using them, with the express purpose of causing harm to other children.

Parents were called in.

A few weeks later, the same Mohammed brought in a mini dagger, on a key ring, attached to his pencil case. The children in class were gathered around his table admiring it. I admired it too, and said that it was very realistic and made of metal and could possibly be used to hurt someone, if we weren't careful, accidently. I firmly suggested that I keep it safe until end of day, when he could have it back, and under no circumstances should he bring it to school again. He was nodding while I was speaking, so I thought he understood my meaning.

A few days later, I noticed the children thronged around Mohammed in the corridor. He had another mini dagger attached to his pencil case. I calmly removed it and told him that he was not getting this one back. Then I reiterated the message of no weapons at school to the whole class and asked one of the sensible girls to translate for me.

"Does everyone understand? These things are dangerous." The children nodded. And that was, I thought, the end of that.

Not so. A few days later the same boy was surrounded by interested classmates and I knew something was going on.

116

"Show me your bag," I said like I was border security.

I checked pockets and zips. There appeared to be nothing. Then one of the other boys said "He have a bag inside, Miss". Sure enough, there was a zip inside a pocket that I hadn't checked and inside there, was about thirty mini daggers, still in their wrapping, ready to be sold to children in the class. I felt like I had just discovered a haul of weapons of mass destruction.

Parents were called. The child was suspended. Again.

Later in the school year, around the middle of May, temperatures were beginning to sky-rocket and the hot desert wind was relentless. The heat and the wind combined, seemed to be affecting the group mood around school and sending even the good kids spastic. (On the up side, this hot dry spell was wonderful for drying washing. A t-shirt was bone dry in under five minutes; a bath towel, around fifteen.) The students didn't want to be at school anymore and neither did the teachers. Everyone was over being there, yet still the spectre of exams and reports hung over us all. We were all a bit frayed round the edges and my personal fuse was unbelievably short.

I would snap at kids who asked me anything, and come down way too hard on any misdemeanor, however trivial. It was unacceptable. It was unprofessional. It was the heat. It was the kids. It was the end. I gave myself a regular talking to – "Just hang on for a few more weeks OK? Keep your head down. Do your fucking job. Stay sane, damn it!"

The children in my class were counting down to the end as much as I was, but possibly at a more subconscious level. The trouble makers had sucked the good kids into their vortex of chaos and no class management strategy seemed to work anymore. The children had regressed to day one, term one and I found myself having to march them up and down corridors in single file because they seemed to have forgotten even basic procedures. They were far too loud and unruly to have in the classroom.

"We are going to do this until everyone gets it right!" I barked.

"Stand straight. One behind the other. No talking. Don't lean on the wall. Don't touch anyone."

"Miss, it's lunchtime," bleated one of the girls.

"I don't care!" I bellowed. "No-one is going to lunch until you show me a tidy, straight, quiet line!"

I was horrible. I was an ogre.

Then, one time, when I was demanding a straight and quiet line outside the classroom, I decided to turn them round for a single file tour of the school. I marched them up the corridor and round the corner just in time to see a chemistry teacher restraining a very large secondary student, surrounded by a mob of other very large boys, who were baying for blood.

"Stop!" I ordered. "Turn round. Walk back to class. No-one speak."

I'm not sure who from my class witnessed the scene. I hope none. It was hard to tell.

Graffiti started to appear on walls around the school - *yuo wal di* – wrongly spelt, but the message was clear. Who was it for? Who will die and how? Would I be murdered in this crazy nut-house for violent offenders? I just had to hang on for a few more weeks, but time was dragging and the end seemed a long way off.

"If you think it's bad now, just wait until the end of term," said Frances at the end of a particularly trying day. "The secondary kids come in, do their exams, then spend the rest of the day smashing up the school and each other."

Oh joy. I could hardly wait.

9

Haram

The children in Tessa's year one class were learning about food. She had managed to get them all settled on the carpet and quiet, long enough for her to introduce the topic *What do we eat?*, which she had written on the whiteboard.

"What do we eat?" she said, while she pointed emphatically at the words.

"Now you try," she encouraged.

"What do we eat?" chimed in the intrigued six year olds, a few of them wriggling and poking each other, one rolling over while another attempted to suck on his shoe. Tessa spent a bit more time on expectations of how to sit and listen and not touch your friend or put anything in your mouth. Then, knowing she had but the briefest of moments before attention drifted away, Tessa had prepared a bag of plastic food items: some of them she had inherited from the trunk left to her by the previous year one teacher. She then explained what she was going to do and that when she pulled something out of the bag, no-one was to move or stand up or make a sound and that everyone was to stay sitting quietly and sensibly. She asked the children what they thought might be in the bag. Most of the children stared blankly or looked around the room, but a couple of hands went up.

"Car," said one boy.

"No, but good word."

"Car," said another boy.

"No," repeated Tessa, shaking her head to reinforce her meaning. Then she pointed again to the question on the whiteboard, while performing a mime of eating something.

"Let's see what is in the bag," she said as she reached in with one hand, feeling around as she did so, to increase the sense of drama.

By now, her collection of children were all squashing round to see and were clambering over each other, to get a better look. There was another pause in the lesson as order was restored, before Tessa revealed the first item from the bag, which was a plastic apple.

Before she could ask the question the class was filled with the shouts of thirty excited voices.

"APPLE! APPLE! APPLE!"

"Yes, yes. Very good. It's an apple," Tessa said as she struggled to regain calm and get through until break time without losing it. She took a deep breath and pulled out the next food item, which was a plastic slice of bacon.

What followed was a split second of stunned silence. The children sat wide eyed and stared at what their teacher held up between her forefinger and thumb. There was an audible intake of breath, before the whole class screamed out "HARAM!"

"Yes, yes, ham," said Tessa, pleased at the children's vocabulary and knowledge of food items.

"HARAM! HARAM!" cried the children again, but this time gesticulating in a display of mild panic.

"Ham. Ham," said Tessa, sensing all was not well. "It's bacon really, but ham is a good word to use."

It was around about the time when, she said these words out loud, that she realised she had unwittingly made a huge cultural faux pas and quickly hid the offensive plastic bacon out of sight.

Haram is a word you hear a lot. It roughly translates to *sin* and can apply to pretty much anything that is perceived as against the teachings of the Qu'ran. In a country where religion rules and there is no distinction between civil law and religious law, a teacher needs to be aware of daily protocols, to get through the day without causing offense and landing oneself in it.

I was not really prepared for cultural bridges that needed to be crossed. I knew about covering up and dressing demurely and that was about it; but there was a whole raft of things I had to be aware of, to avoid *haram*. To guide us in our teaching practice and possible cultural offense, we were given a list of 31 points to keep in mind from the Ministry of Education to read and file: reference to 'the eating of pigs' was on this list.

What surprised me about Tessa's *ham* incident was that the six year old children all knew what the plastic bacon represented. They could identify that it was haram, indicating that they had come across it before in a learning experience. Perhaps, in a reception class, there had been a similar lesson involving sinful things to be avoided for five year olds. Maybe, the teacher had pulled out this same piece of plastic bacon and told her class sternly that it was haram and that it was from a pig that was also haram, and that under no circumstances were they to think of these sinful things as food and that if they did, they would go straight to hell.

Other points on the ministry's haram list were historical or geographical. Israel could not be named and had been eliminated from all the world maps in school with a black marker pen. Anything to do with Israel, the Jews, Hitler's persecution and the holocaust were off limits. We were to avoid talking about the Quran, Allah or the prophet Mohammed. We were to steer clear of any religious connotations, political thinking or cultural relevance at all. We could not use books that alleged that religion was at the heart of any conflict, such as the crusades of the Middle Ages or that Islam was spread by force. We were expressly told not to teach Darwin's theory of natural selection or evolution. We could not use books which were linked to witchcraft, magic, reincarnation or the 'transmigration of souls'. Reference to the consumption of alcohol or drug use was banned and the Arabian Gulf was never to be referred to as the Persian Gulf.

Sandra and her learning support team were given the job of going through all the newly arrived texts and reading books. She was given a list of pages to be altered or removed completely from each book. Armed with black markers, the team of five women located the offending content and struck it out, making the reading material palatable for consumption by children at school.

One of these books was *Six Dinner Sid*, a favourite story of mine to read aloud as a shared book. It tells of a cat that lives simultaneously at six houses in his street, and so he gets fed six dinners. All the people in the street believe that the cat is theirs, exclusively, and call him by different names. It is a wonderful story, beautifully illustrated.

One day after lunch, I settled my class on the floor in the library and started to read from a big book of *Six Dinner Sid*, holding it up so the children could see the pictures. All was going well until the page where we learn Sid's different names. Caramouche is the first one, then it's Bob, then it's Satan, which to my alarm had been blacked out.

The children became immediately intrigued and asked why someone had drawn in the book. Thinking quickly, I said the name of the cat was Sultan, a name common in Arabic countries. I muttered something about how it is bad to draw in books, then swiftly turned the page and continued with the story.

Other books in the class book corner and library were similarly altered. One of the readers, *Traditional Stories from Around the World*, was extremely on the thin side because the creation stories were torn out. And seemingly innocent topics in literacy had to be rethought because of the haram content: *Myths and Legends* was just *Legends* and the exploits of the ancient Greeks was null and void. In fact, all the classical cultural references that shape the British curriculum went out of the window.

In secondary, the science curriculum was full of haram pitfalls that had to be negotiated. Somehow, the children had to make sense of the world, without the framework of the Big Bang theory or evolution. The history of dinosaurs was tolerated, but there is no way that people could ever have developed from single-celled bacteria in primordial slime. According to Kuwaiti science, people were simply made out of mud by God. End of story.

There was no sex ed. Teachers could not refer to male and female parts in biology. It was all haram.

In life outside school, the Kuwaiti public were protected from prolific haram images, especially in women's magazines, by the diligence of the permanent black marker of censorship. Each magazine on any shelf in supermarkets or corner shops had been carefully monitored and any womanly cleavage, thigh or upper arm was blacked out. Pages showing women's fashion were comedic in the sanctified vandalism, where a sexy plunging neckline was tidily coloured in, so as not to offend. Well-known celebrities and models with black-pen modified outfits, made a mockery of seductive smiles and pouts to the camera. Some magazines with a double page spread of red-carpet arrivals, were reduced to a collection of heads, hands and feet, linked together with black felt-tip blobs.

To save the nation's moral fiber, the Ministry of Censorship was at its most noticeable at the movies, where haram content was ruthlessly removed. Violence was left in, but anything remotely racy was hacked away. For example, *The Wolf of Wall Street*, with an original running time of three hours was reduced for Kuwaiti consumption to two hours, ten minutes.

Censorship was everywhere, like Big Brother watching. At school and at home, there were certain internet sites where an 'access denied' message was annoyingly displayed. It was disappointing not to be able to show some useful educational documentaries, from the likes of *BBC kids* and the schools' relevant resources pages. Although, there was a way to bypass the block on YouTube.

During a lesson about Britain, I clicked on a link for *English country garden*, the famous song set to a montage of colourful English gardens. The photos showed cutsey cottage gardens and formal clipped hedges of stately homes. There were roses trailing from bowers and bursts of daisies and sunflowers, as the song pom-pom-diddli-ommed. The children watched the imagery and seemed genuinely interested in Elizabethan revival and Gothic stonework of the Victorian herbaceous border. Everything was peaceful and I only had to separate a couple of boys, who had decided to use their pencils as weapons.

Then suddenly, a roar went up. Children screamed, pointed at the screen and shouted "HARAM! HARAM!"

I reached for the mouse and quickly paused the film. It took me a while to calm the children and find out just what had happened to upset them. They were extremely excited; some of them jumping up and down, others rolling around on the carpet laughing uncontrollably.

126

The sinful, upsetting image from the seemingly innocent montage was the back view of a reclining male nude – bum clearly visible through a drapery of ivy.

On another occasion, during a science lesson, I played a film clip to illustrate the states of matter. The voice-over was explaining that the air we breathe is a gas, and that even though we can't see it, it is as real and present as the water in the ocean and the sand and rocks beneath our feet. Then, uh-oh, the camera panned down from the clouds in the summer sky, to a family playing in the waves and digging in the sand, in their western style swim wear. A gasp erupted in my class, from the shock of seeing flesh and I lunged for the TV remote 'off' button, deflecting attention from the film content with the question "Who can name the three states of matter?"

I realised then, that all content had to be scanned for haram.

It wasn't only content from books and film that had the potential for cultural offense. A boy in class was making a noise by folding and unfolding a piece of paper. He was not paying attention and the continual action and noise was distracting the class away from me.

"Put it away or in the bin," I hissed, low and menacing. He looked at me wide-eyed and did not move. "Ahmed. The bin. Now."

"Is haram," said Ahmed quietly.

"Do it," I insisted, indicating the large plastic receptacle by the classroom door with a nod of the head.

"It has the name of Ala," he replied.

"Why do you have Ala's stuff? Put it away or in the bin. It is distracting others and annoying me," I persist.

"But is haram."

"Yes, yes," chime in the rest of the class, "haram, haram, haram."

"Ok then, give it back to Ala. And Ala," I turn to address Ala who looked at me equally quizzically, "put it away."

I was puzzled at this stage, because I couldn't work out why it was a sin to throw Ala's paper in the rubbish. Ala was a boy in the class and he clearly had no use for the, by now, scrunched up piece of paper.

Then it dawned on me. The piece of paper was from the Islamic teacher and had the name of Allah printed on it, not Ala. The piece of paper was therefore sacred and could not possibly be thrown away as a piece of rubbish. That would most certainly have been haram. Teaching was proving to be a minefield of potential sin.

After a while of living in Kuwait, the cultural complexities that seem unusual on arrival seep into your life and start to become normal. I noticed this one day, when I took my regular trip to the supermarket at Al Kout and was shocked to see some western women flaunting their upper arms and uncovered legs with shameless disregard for their own nakedness. I can only imagine the disgust and alarm felt by the good Muslims of the neighbourhood. Haram! Haram! Haram!

10

At home

Ah, the Ivory Tower. We called it the Ivory Tower, partly because it was the top floor apartment and partly because the walls, floor tiles and ceiling were shades of white. Ah, my heavenly haven. My safe place, away from the mess and madness; above the noise and chaos of outside. Coming home was always like coming home. Unlocking the door and stepping through to tranquility and Zen, I could finally breathe and relax. I would dump bags, kick off sandals, swap work clothes for lounge wear, put the kettle on, allow my hair to do what it wanted. Sanity returning with my equilibrium. Yes. Breathe. And there in the afternoon sun, my sofa. Comfy. As welcoming as a hug, I would fall into its embrace then stretch out like a cat, smiling all the way to my toes. Yeah. And do nothing.

It was a Thursday evening at the Ivory Tower. I was celebrating the end of another week at the coal face, with a glass of home-made red and a David Attenborough documentary about birds - a guilty pleasure. I was enjoying myself immensely, when the peace was shattered by a sound like a giant, emptying a giant-sized wheelbarrow load of gravel. It shook me and my lounge. 'Uh-oh,' I thought.

I paused David and went to investigate.

Outside my window, I could see the remains of a building that had been empty for some time and was in the process of being demolished. Now I could see the reason for the giant gravelly sound. Through the clearing dust, I could make out the derelict apartment building, which had crumpled and slumped under its own weight. Its flat roof was now a steep ramp and masonry was scattered in chunks and bits, all over the road.

I heard sirens. Emergency vehicles were arriving, noisy with flashing lights and a crowd had started to gather, as people do when they sense disaster. I scurried up to the roof for a better view.

From my new vantage point I watched the drama unfold. Police, firemen and ambulance personnel milled about, gathering in clusters for a brief discussion, before climbing about on the broken building, shining torches and taking selfies. More vehicles with flashing lights arrived. It must have been a slow night for the emergency services as all units seemed to have shown up here. This was the hottest ticket in town. I watched and sipped my wine waiting for the heroic rescues to begin. More blokes in uniform appeared with tool belts and cell phones, certainly looking the part, but not actually doing anything. There were two or three who were obviously there to record the proceedings with movie cameras and sound equipment.

There was more milling about, then some men in yellow hard hats posed for a group pic in the style of a sports team: some standing in a row, some crouching down in front, all smiles. There didn't seem to be any urgency in what they were doing. Certainly, if there was anyone trapped in the collapsed building, they would have to wait for the team building exercise to finish before they were dug out and lifted to safety. I assumed that there was no-one to rescue and I soon lost interest in this grown up version of *Kidzania*. I went back downstairs to my couch to resume watching David.

Apartment buildings grow and die like field mushrooms, in Kuwait, and I get the feeling that quality is not uppermost in a developer's mind when constructing the country's high-rise dwellings. Our apartment building was new, we were told. And although it had newish features, such as ceramic tiles and not-quite-finished power sockets, there were certain aspects that were absolutely second hand. The kitchen cupboards, that I scrubbed in an attempt to remove someone else's grease, grime and pumpkin soup, were definitely not new, and the bath had a coin-sized hole in the enamel.

All around the neighbourhood, apartment blocks were being built, briefly inhabited before being pulled down. This semi-permanence contributed to feeling of living on a building site, that would never be not a building site.

The various apartment building sites around our neighbourhood were hazardous places. Sure, there was visible signage for worker safety, indicating steel-capped boots and hard hats to be worn at all times. But the real picture was immigrant labourers wearing flipflops and lungi, swinging from bundles of timber or buckets of cement, suspended from a crane with no head protection apart from a loosely tied turban. The scaffolding appeared rickety and roped together and everyone seemed to be smoking on the job.

In the news media there were regular reports of deaths on the 2022 soccer world cup stadium in Qatar. In Kuwait, as in Qatar and other Arabic countries, immigrant labour is cheap and plentiful and there is no worker representative body regulating construction safety conditions. Again, I am reminded of the third world aspect of these uber-rich states.

You didn't have to be a qualified building inspector to identify the serious shortfalls of the school building. The place was a construction nightmare of corners that didn't quite fit together, tangles of wire spewing out of holes in the wall and tile work, especially in the toilets, which could have featured on D.I.Y. disasters. Everything about the physical building was shoddy and ugly and I wondered how the parents, with their huge amounts of wealth, could possibly be okay about sending their children here, day after day.

As a learning environment, the school definitely did not deliver. The classrooms were too small for the number of children, and most of them did not have adequate natural lighting. The general atmosphere was highly impersonal and unwelcoming. There was not nearly enough outside space for children to let off steam and run around. This single factor was, in my mind, the biggest contributor to the violence and behaviour issues we had to put up with.

The contrast of this place, to the schools in New Zealand, where there are swathes of green playing fields and shade-giving leafy trees, was laughably sad. Here, the whole school of fifteen hundred children shared a space, the size of a basketball court, for P.E. and all breaks. There was, however, an Astroturf soccer pitch we could use in the Arabic school next door, but half way through the year this was ripped up and the school demolished in preparation for a new school building. The new school building turned out to be a carbon copy of the existing one. No thought had been wasted on how to improve the learning environment or how to create a more user friendly space. It was just the same; painted in the same shit brown.

During the build, some secondary P.E. lessons happened in a rented playing field two blocks away. As far as I could tell, everyone had complained about the woeful lack of outside space and how this impacted on the children. The issue had become a political football between management and staff, so this meager concession and paltry expense for the rented field, was a small triumph.

The environment at school was clearly toxic and potentially lethal, so it was no real surprise when Sandra, one day before school, had excitedly knocked at the door and smugly hinted that we most probably would get the day off. She had just heard from Rupert, that the school had been damaged by the storm in the night and that part of the masonry had come loose, and some of it had crashed onto the quad.

"The school can't possibly stay open," she said. "It's way too dangerous. What if a child gets hit by falling bricks?"

"Yipee," was my response and we skipped down the road, greeting the dead cat with hearty grins, like characters in *The Wizard of Oz*. When we got to school, however, it was a different story. Masonry had indeed been dislodged from the roof and chunks of brick were still being cleared from the tiled floor of the quad, but to my dismay, no closure had been called.

Management had decided that children would be safe, as long as they stayed in their classrooms, so any P.E. and break-time was cancelled for the day. Repairs would be done during the day and the quad was strictly out of bounds. This was the worst outcome possible, as the children didn't do well in the confined space of the classroom all day, and that meant that I wouldn't be getting a break either. I wished for the school to fall down properly and be done with it. But, alas, it was patched up and stayed standing.

Cheap apartments blocks, shoddy construction and broken mud brick houses - this was the building standard in Mangaf and the outer edges of the city. On the roads towards the city centre, in more uptown areas, the cheap apartment blocks thin out and grand private homes dominate the landscape. These homes are fortresses for the occupants. Each one built borrowing from various disparate styles. Here's one, the colour of lemon icing on a French Fancy; here's another with Kremlin-type onion towers; there's one that looks like a Disney palace; and one that could be a Bond villain's lair. There's one that owes much to Italian baroque with marble figures adorning the roof, and one that looks like Versailles behind decorative wrought iron gates. There's one that has turrets that remind me of Little Gem biscuits from my childhood, and one straight out of the *Arabian Nights*. There are some which would not be out of place along the Californian coast and some which look like they have been transplanted from a Bavarian forest.

As private homes these places are enormous and have been built with very little space in between and very little outside living area. Unlike western homes, where a certain amount of land square footage is reserved for a garden or yard, nearly all the land is taken up with house. There are large gates and high walls street side. The windows seal with pull-down shutters because of regular sand storms and front doors appear as a barrier to entry, rather than a welcoming way in. Security cameras are everywhere.

The architectural legacies of statement public buildings are few. The famous Kuwaiti Towers, water towers designed by Danish/Swedish and built by Yugoslavs (as was then) in the seventies, are brave, futuristic land marks, with a space age feel. There is a revolving restaurant inside one of the glittering blue orbs, which is skewered to the tallest of the three spikes, but unfortunately this was closed for renovation when I was there.

The other piece of architecture worth noting is the Grand Mosque at the centre of Kuwait City, which boasts of a capacity of ten thousand worshippers, under a forty-three metre high dome. Although this incredibly huge space of prayer was finished in 1986, at a cost of fourteen million Kuwaiti dinar, a further eight million was spent on renovation in 2013, for 'structural problems'. I visited with a group of teachers from school. It was certainly huge and magnificent in a ritzy glitzy way, but there was something amiss when our guide said, with pride, that the mosque was 'almost thirty years old'. 'Really?' I thought, as my mind conjured images of medieval stone churches of Europe, still standing after hundreds of years of wear and tear. Longevity is relative: in Kuwait thirty is old for a building.

Kuwait City is dominated by cars. The roads and highways are laid out as if there might be some town planning, with street lighting and curb stones, but there seems to be very little thought regarding community or shared public space. There are vacant lots, which people use as running tracks and sports grounds for cricket and football. These spaces are also used as bus parks and rubbish tips for construction and households. Walking across such a space I would find discarded plastic toys, bundles of tie-wire, tyres, car batteries, coat-hangers, a lounge suite, breeze-blocks, piles of rubble, reinforcing steel rods, a number of dead cats and rats, broken pallets, bags of rubbish and wrecked vehicles. One time, there was even an abandoned, full-size theatre set, complete with an elaborate proscenium arch, a curved staircase and plum coloured satin curtains. Tessa took a photo of some dismembered shop window mannequins; weirdly calm, made up faces and contorted limbs, eerily human. Two fifty-seater buses lay side by side, torched and dead, like beached whales or a teenage suicide pact. This was a no-man's land reminiscent of a post apocalyptic scene from *Mad Max*.

Across the road from the Ivory Tower a burnt out car had become a hangout for group of immigrant workers. They had dragged some discarded furniture over and sat there comfortably smoking cigarettes, while watching their mates play cricket: the car carcass serving as a sort of clubhouse.

I noticed other uses for home furnishings: a queen-size mattress had cleverly been wired on to a garage wall to fill a hole; a green velour covered arm-chair was put to use as a traffic cone in the middle of a road, where some subsidence had occurred, next to a building site; pieces of carpet were used, in an attempt to fill in potholes.

Mohammed, the caretaker in our building, had been drinking. He stood in the doorway to the Ivory Tower hands on hips, elbows sticking out like wings, eyes half-closed and bleary.

"Your water. Is ok?" he drawled before blowing cigarette smoke out of the side of his mouth, the way cigarette smokers do in the presence of non-smokers; as if the smoke is somehow less obnoxious if it come out sideways.

Tessa and I paused, forks halfway to mouths and looked at him. We were having a picnic style, take-away dinner on the lounge carpet. There had been a knock at the door and neither of us could be bothered getting up, so we just shouted "Come in!" thinking it was Sandra or Dave, or another of our teacher neighbours. This, I greatly regretted because now, Mohammed was standing in the doorway. He was swaying a little as he took another puff of his fag.

Tessa, being the more polite of us, got up and had a look at the taps in the kitchen, while I yelled, so even someone with minimal English would understand, "GET OUT!!!"

Mohammed had been handy with a broken tap in the kitchen and, rather more seriously, a blocked toilet in the bathroom. He was a good sort though, and didn't complain when we told him about our *mushkala.*

"No Kleenex in, ok?" he said, clutching a bin liner of poo and toilet paper that he had extracted from our loo. Yes, we understood now that the plumbing in Kuwait wasn't designed for western habits and that all paper had to go in a bin, to be deposited in one of the skips on the street outside.

Rupert and Sandra learnt that lesson too and poor Mohammed was called in to unblock their loo too. Without gloves or any protective wear at all, he rolled up his sleeves and pulled out fistfuls of shit, heaving it into plastic bags. He then tried to budge the wedge of the blockage with caustic soda, which turned out to be part of a house brick.

"My hands, they hurt, it's burning!" he said, with a good-natured smile.

Sandra and Rupert hid at our place until the stink had almost gone. It took a while. Several cups of tea, open windows and sticks of incense later, it was safe for them to return home across the hall.

Mohammed was harmless enough. Even when he was drunk and smoking in our lounge he was okay. It was Tessa that had been friendly with Mohammed, stopping by to chat sometimes while waiting for the lift. He had been teaching her some useful Arabic words and phrases, but as usual with men in any place on the planet, he had taken this all the wrong way and perceived her quest for language as flirtation. Hence, the enquiry about our plumbing, the happy drunken swaying and casual cigarette smoking in our lounge.

Dave had also been chatting with Mohammed and learning useful Arabic words and phrases. Always thinking, he had taken the precaution of having a photo of himself with Mohammed and Mohammed's friend. They were all wearing dishdashas and grinning, thumbs up, like chums who had known each other for a long time. He had this photo handily in his phone incase, he said, Islamic extremists came to call. He would show them the photo as evidence he was friend to the Muslim, and would therefore not be tortured, executed or beheaded.

Mohammed had been encouraged by the friendliness of Tessa and Dave and sometimes he would arrive at the door unannounced: he knocked and then just let himself in.

"You are teacher," he said in his usual jovial manner.

"Yes," I said toweling my hair.

Tessa stopped typing and looked up from her laptop.

There was a brief moment of confusion before Mohammed stepped aside to allow a woman, who was fully veiled, accompanied by a teenage boy who was smiling brightly, to enter our humble abode.

"She want teacher for the son," Mohammed explained.

Tessa and I looked at each other, then at the woman and boy. There was an awkward pause.

"We are teachers, but at school. Not at home," I said slowly and carefully.

We all blinked at each other for a minute or two, then Mohammed ushered his visitors out.

"Maybe the other teachers," he said smiling, waving his hand above his head as he left. I think at this point and with no prompting from me, Tessa decided to distance herself from our friendly caretaker.

There was an unexpected bomb-shell half-way through the second term.

"All teachers will have to vacate the new apartments by the end of this month," said Cliff in a stiff, but apologetic tone.

"Shit, I didn't see that coming," mumbled Tessa in a sideways whisper.

We were, of course, devastated. Why? Why? Why? No! No! No! Not fair! Not fair! Not fair! The idea of not going home to the Ivory Tower was an unbelievable nightmare. The Ivory Tower was my refuge; my reward at the end of the day; my safe place. How was I going to cope? Our light and airy peaceful space of tranquility and calm would be cruelly taken away from us and we were expected to move into the dark and infinitely inferior old teachers' building. Ugh. I was suddenly tired at the prospect and cried inside. All the teachers in the new building were assigned their apartment numbers in the old teachers' building, and the exodus began.

A collection of the school's maintenance and labouring personnel arrived with a flatbed utility vehicle. Each apartment was emptied; furniture was dismantled, loaded onto the van then reassembled in the allocated space. Each pair of occupants to be moved were told when it would be their turn. I was shocked that my colleagues seemed absolutely fine with a double whammy of inconvenience - 1) to be moving at all, and 2) to be moving on a precious weekend.

I voiced my concerns to Tessa. Clearly we had to go, but we were definitely not moving out on our time. We cleverly arranged our moving day to be a Sunday and the final day of eviction. I messaged Cliff Saturday night to arrange cover for our classes, sad but quietly smug that we had wangled a day off work for shifting our stuff.

Our new flat was clean enough. I had made a list of things that needed doing and, sure enough on inspection before the move, they had been attended to. All, except the removal of the curtains, which looked like they had never been taken down and cleaned, since the day they were put up. They hung in elaborate swags, with tassels and tie-backs in matching fabric: an opulent style which would not have looked out of place in Miss Haversham's dusty mansion. I felt that by taking them down, we would destroy a micro-biotic ecosystem worthy of a BBC documentary and possible voice over by David Attenborough.

The generous proportions of floor space that we had enjoyed at the Ivory Tower, were cut to about a third. We ditched the dining table and six chairs, as well as the coffee table. The bedroom furniture just about fit into the only just adequate bedrooms, and only really worked in one configuration.

In the stairwell of our new address, I discovered a store of disused lounge furniture. I grabbed a whole heap of newish cushions which made up the seats and backs of arm chairs, and dusted off some small low tables. We took down the curtains ourselves, because it became too hard to explain to the hired help what we wanted them to do: they couldn't seem to understand how we could possibly not want the curtains!

Hired help/ handyman: Why you no want? (pointing to the curtains).

Me: Because very dirty (making an unhappy face, shaking my head).

Hired help/ handyman: (Seems puzzled. Says something in Tamil to his buddy.)

Me: They have to go (I mime pulling curtains and throwing them out of the door).

Handyman's buddy: Why you no want?

Me: You like. You take.

Hired help/ handyman and his buddy look at each other and smile like the white lady has gone mad.

The school labourers/ handy men and maids inhabited the old teachers' building too, but in the basement. Unlike the teaching staff, they had to pay for their accommodation. This was the difference, I

142

decided, between *expats* and *immigrants*: an expat was on a contract with a package which generally included flights, accommodation and utilities, where as an immigrant arrived and took their chances, through friends or family contacts, on the job market.

Immigrants in Kuwait seemed to fall into two main categories depending on their country of origin. At school, the work of cleaners and maids was done by Indian, Sri Lankan and Bangladeshi women. The security staff were Filipino women. The labourers/ handy men were also from the Indian subcontinent and because they were on the payroll, anything that needed fixing was done by them: no need to contract specialists, when there was an army of personnel standing by ready to botch a job. The untrained, on-site handy men probably went some way to explain the general shoddiness of school and the strange and wonderful things that happened regarding electricity and plumbing, at home.

I never went down to the basement. I was never invited and I didn't feel comfortable stepping into the private world below stairs. There was no lock on the door and after a violent storm one day, there was no door; but I felt I would have been intruding, to venture down there. I learned from the people who lived there that the space was divided into small cubicles, with a cot in each for the single workers. Married immigrants with families made their own arrangements, often living with relatives, in the run-down, soon-to-be-condemned apartment blocks nearby.

I felt a twinge of guilt when I found out what the maids earned, knowing that, unlike the teaching staff, there were no perks. Close to the start of the school year, the maids held a strike for more pay. They had been promised an increase on their monthly wage from eighty KD to one hundred, for a five day week of nine hours a day. The women gathered one afternoon in the quad, as a show of solidarity. Om Mohammed, the self-appointed maid wrangler, shouted at them to get back to their stations. When they didn't comply with her commands, she confiscated their handbags and harangued them some more, telling them that they would all be fired and replaced if they caused any more trouble.

The situation was finally resolved when the maids accepted the management's offer of one hundred KD, but with extended work hours of a whole extra day, which meant their hourly rate was reduced, but at least they got their twenty KD increase. The women returned to work and were given back their handbags.

As a teacher, I was most definitely an expat and not an immigrant. I look like a teacher. I have been born lucky: the right colour, in the right place, speaking the right language. I am one of the fortunates in the *haves* category of life. In Kuwait, the segregation between the *haves* and the *have-nots* is alive and well, and not viewed as an embarrassment or a social issue to be fixed. There are the rich people who are in charge, who need poor people to do the menial tasks and things they, rich people, don't want to do themselves. It is just the way things are.

144

At our apartment, once the curtains were down and the carpet was rolled out, the little space we had was fully maximized and was quite pleasing and comfortable. I removed some light-bulbs to soften the lighting, creating an overall effect of a floor-level, cushioned shisha cafe or opium den.

As we moved into our new pad, the pair of three-seater sofas were eyed up by one of the other teachers in the building. I said they were up for grabs, which she was pleased about, and they were installed in her apartment downstairs. This seemed straight forward enough at the time, but this decision was revisited at the end of the year with the announcement of an apartment inspection.

We had a list of all the furnishings that should have been in each apartment. Each item was to be ticked off by a school representative in order to receive one hundred KD that was held back from our final pay. The admin staff had conveniently forgotten that we had decided not to bring the furniture from the Ivory Tower to fill our tiny lounge. On the last day before we all flew out I approached the admin office with the list to try and sort things out.

"In order to receive the one hundred KD, you must replace the furniture," said Ms Huda matter-of-factly, peering at me over her glasses as she leaned on a mountain of paper and folders on her desk.

I stepped out of the office to process this information. With only a few hours to go before flying out, was I really going to find our furniture and shift it in to the apartment? I knew the two sofas were in an apartment downstairs, but I had no idea where the removal men had stacked the rest of the furniture from the Ivory Tower. Answer: no. I stepped back into Ms Huda's office.

"What about if you sign to say it's all there. I mean it's not actually in the apartment, but the furniture is somewhere," I said, trying to smile, but knowing my face was betraying me.

There was a moment where I believed this plan was not going to be acceptable. I held out the tick sheet in my hand appealing to the gods of logic and common sense. We stared at each other, weighing up the this-verses-that scenarios: I could see her point and she could see mine. After a minute, she made a call and gabbled in Arabic, then said the magic words "It's done. Hallas," and made the international sign of being done with something – two brisk movements, slapping the right hand over the left, then repeating with left hand over right before holding up both hands, arms bent at the elbow, palms facing forward. She grabbed the piece of paper, gave it a scribble and nodded to the next door office, where a man in a suit was handing out cash.

11

Health and Fitness

There was an emergency meeting in the theatre after school.

"As many of you have already heard, there is the potential of an epidemic of swine flu: the H1N1 strain," said Cliff earnestly. "Please make sure you take this document from the ministry, and sign for it, on your way out. Thank you, have a great weekend."

There had been reports from Qatar of two children who had died from this particular flu virus, so all schools in the Middle East were now on high alert.

My immediate thought was, I'm ashamed to say, not concern for the parents and families of the deceased, but a faint glimmer of hope that somehow the school would be closed due to the spread of this highly infectious disease.

The document read as follows:-

Subject: Dealing with H1N1

Implementing to the attached letter from undersecretary assistant for general education regarding the above subject.

Please instruct to all the (educational and administrative staff) to abide instructions stated as follows:-

1. *To appoint an officer to deal with this case.*

2. *Identify the medical center (clinic) which located at the school area, and had been allocated by the ministry of health to deal with flu cases.*

3. *Restrict use of emergency numbers, medical center's numbers, and the number of the head of the medical center if possible.*

4. *The officer to be aware in case of suspected cases of the disease, and to perform the following actions:-*

> — *Immediate access to the head of medical center (clinic), and inform of the situation, and to take necessary action for the patient.*

> — *Request a medical team to examine the location.*

> — *To instruct to sterilize all places (all classes and educational facilities).*

> — *Educate staff how to prevent infection of (H1N1).*

All staff to sign their knowledge of the newsletter, and a legal action will be taken against anyone who violates this.

As I read the words, I recognised it as English and kind of understood the gist, but I'm still not one hundred per cent sure of its exact meaning.

The flu saga continued at flag ceremony one day the following week, when Cliff made one of his inspirational speeches.

"I'd like to share with you all a story," he began. "A boy came to me yesterday, and do you know what he said? He said to me 'thank you'."

"'Thank you? I said. But why are you thanking me?' I said to him."

"And do you know what he said then? He said 'because you have given us hand sanitizer and that shows that the school cares about our health.'"

Hand sanitizer dispensers had indeed popped up in various locations around the school, although ordinary soap in the toilets was still a rationed commodity: sometimes there, sometimes not, often running out, sometimes replaced. But now there was hand sanitizer, a replacement for soap? I'm not sure.

One of these new plastic dispensers that was handily located on the wall in the quad at the bottom of a busy stairwell, didn't seem to be working. Children were furiously pulling on the plastic handle, but no gooey liquid was coming out. The children's frustrations were noticed by Frances, a concerned teacher. She opened the dispenser in an effort to discover the fault, only to find that the plastic bag containing the hand sanitizer liquid was still sealed. On enquiry she was told by Om Mohammed, the head of the maids, school dictator and resident ogre, that it would be opened 'only for when ministry come'.

Like the virus, rumours were now flying around. Stories of eight cases of H1N1 were said to be confirmed at a school in Hawally, and yet that school remained open. Five reported cases should have shut the school down in order to contain the spread of the disease. The assumption fueling the rumours was that the school was not reporting its cases to the ministry, to avoid a panic in the school.

At our school, we had been told to send any child we suspected of having symptoms directly to the school doctor, although children in my class tried to take full advantage of this opportunity to get out of lessons. The doctor's office had a desk, a filing cabinet, a narrow treatment bed and posters on the wall depicting sad looking children in bandages, the pulmonary system and some marketing material from Dettol. There was an office with a sign on the door, but for a while, no medical practitioner. This post was temporarily held by the aforementioned Om Mohammed. Om Mohammed means Mother of Mohammed, a fairly common name in the Arabic world. Here in school she was a force of nature.

Sandra had noticed a boy in year three who was not feeling well. He said he had a sore tummy and a head ache. She told his teacher that she would take him to the doctor's office as it was on her way to the staff room. As they were about to enter the doctor's office they encountered Om Mohammed who barged through the door, ushered them in, closing the door behind her. Then she carefully put on a white coat that hung on a hook behind the door.

"Yallah," she yelled, beaconing Sandra and the small boy to sit on the treatment bed. Sandra, tried to communicate that maybe the boy just needed to go home and rest, but she felt compelled to stay seated and keep quiet and still.

Om Mohammed hobbled round to the filing cabinet. She had something a-miss with her joints, possibly arthritis, and moved around like she had just been for a really long horse ride. She walked, legs apart, rolling from one foot to the other. She was large and imposing – picture Brian's mum, from the cult classic Monty Python film *Life of*

Brian. At break times she would terrify children with her yelling and threats of violence. She positioned herself on a chair by the snack shop, legs apart, hands leaning on her knees. When she spotted a cute kid from one of the year one classes, she would scoop it up and sit it on her lap. The poor child dare not move and would sit rigid with fear until released back onto the quad. Later in the year she would be conspicuous by her absence because she had somehow run over her own foot. She had to wear a cast for some time.

It was her voice that I remember most about Om Mohammed. Once, early on, I made the mistake of putting my finger to my lips in the international sign for 'Shhhhhhh', while she was berating some maids in the corridor. Without slowing down or quieting at all, she turned her tidal wave of tumult on me, shaking her head and gesticulating wildly. She had a voice, one colleague poetically noted, that could turn the most virile man impotent.

In the doctor's office, Om Mohammed purposefully yanked open the middle drawer and pulled out a shallow basket filled with medical-looking bottles and jars. She sifted through the contents, muttering in Arabic, occasionally addressing the boy who appeared paralyzed by dread. She grasped a small wooden spatula and a white bottle from the basket, which she rattled playfully before approaching the boy.

"Ahhh," she demonstrated, the international cue to 'open wide', then she stuck the wooden spatula into the boys mouth, pressed it down on his tongue and peered in.

She made some grunts and utterances of wisdom, then she unscrewed the bottle, tipped two large white tablets into her hand then fed them to the boy, who then hopped off the bed and left the room to get a drink of water.

Sandra was now an accomplice to this misdemeanor. Why had she not intervened? Why did she let this woman, who was obviously not a doctor, or even a nurse, or a person with any kind of medical knowledge, potentially poison a child? She doesn't know. Sandra said later that she couldn't quite believe what was happening. It was all very surreal.

When the boy, clearly still alive, came back into the doctor's office, Om Mohammed yelled something at him, and then turned to Sandra and yelled at her "toilet, toilet," while miming a gesture with her hand which could only be interpreted as a lot of poo coming out of her bottom.

During the swine flu episode, a mild panic did develop around school for a while. Children emptied all the available hand sanitizer dispensers and inevitably broke some of them with their ferocious handle pulling. The ministry never came to make an inspection of the directives it had laid out, much to Om Mohammed's disappointment, and the threat of death by a swine flu epidemic became absorbed into the general maelstrom of regular school dramas, and lost its potency.

That was one of the scary realities of this place: that somehow someone, anyone could put on a white coat and be a doctor. And it wasn't only at school. One of the science teachers had unfortunately had to go to hospital because he was experiencing chest pains. At the international hospital he had mentioned to the Indian doctor who examined him, something about the smartness of the nurses' uniforms. The Indian doctor had responded to this observation with "They are not nurses. They are Kuwaiti doctors. Don't let them hear you say that."

Apparently, in this land of delusion, the standard of medical study is so low that graduates of med school can only work in hospitals in Kuwait as 'Kuwaiti doctors'. They do the job of nurses. Any actual doctors are imported to work in private and government run hospitals and healthcare centres.

Free medical treatment was one of the draw-cards of the job advertisement for teachers in Kuwait. But I was here on a tourist visa which meant that I had no access to the free medical treatment from government run healthcare, if I did fall over with an ailment. Free treatment was only available to teachers who had acquired residency and a civil I.D. Attaining civil I.D. required a long, drawn out and expensive process of forms, official stamps and health checks.

Rupert had embarked on this lengthy procedure before arriving in Kuwait with the naïve belief that he needed civil I.D. before he could start work. Silly man. So in the U.K. he had paid for a full medical examination, including a chest x-ray and a blood test. He had started the process, but because the Civil I.D. had not been issued before his departure to start work, he was told, by H.R. at school, that he had to do it all again here, in Kuwait – at his own expense.

So began the drama. First stop – blood test.

One morning, Rupert was informed that a car was waiting for him outside. There were two men in dark suits and shades in the car: a minder who didn't speak much English and a driver who didn't speak at all. Rupert was to be taken to the medical centre where he would get a blood test, then brought back to school. The minder had his passport which he safely tucked behind the sun-visor of the passenger side.

Off they went. Surprisingly for Rupert the car did not join the queue of traffic on the expressway to the city, but took the opposite direction past the refinery and out into the blinding desert. The drive through beige dust, punctuated with pylons and the occasional scrubby tree, came to an end when the car slowed to a stop outside one lonely low-rise building at the side of the road.

"Come," said the minder as he retrieved Rupert's passport. Then he led the way to the door of the building, which turned out to be a medical centre.

Inside, the temperature was stifling. The minder pushed past a line of brown-skinned immigrants who were standing, shirtless. The line extended up some steps and round a corner. Occasionally some men came the other way, still shirtless and pressing wads of cotton-wool against a freshly punctured artery on the right arm. Some of these wads of bloodied wound dressing, Rupert noticed, littered the floor and had been poked into holes in the stair banister. They continued down another corridor and Rupert was shown into an air-conditioned waiting room. He was the only occupant.

After an hour or so, the minder returned and with minimal vocal cues motioned for Rupert to follow. Once again, they pushed past the line of waiting men. He was then asked to remove his shirt before being shown into the doctor's office. The Indian doctor, who spoke excellent English, was efficient and professional. After the blood test, the minder escorted the Rupert back to the car and back to school.

"I really didn't think I was coming back," he admitted later. "All the way out there I was thinking, I should have called the kids, to say good bye."

While I was teaching here in Kuwait, I managed to remain reasonably fit and well. I did, however, endure a permanent itchy throat: the sort of itchiness that bodes doom of a full on flu. The flu does not descend but the itchiness persists. This is desert throat. It is the result of living in a dry, dusty place. The condition is exacerbated by shouting at children, which had I started to do, a lot.

Other teachers had more severe maladies. Myrtle, Deputy Head of Primary, had a raft of ailments and, if you were unlucky enough to meet her in the corridor, she would offer a smorgasbord of updates on her blood-clot, diabetes, frozen-shoulder, respiratory issues and various injuries she had sustained after falling down an uncovered man-hole in Kazakhstan. Sometimes, if I saw her approach, I would feign absentmindedness, turn and walk in the opposite direction.

She would regularly burst into Rupert's office crying or bent double and he, being a kindly man, would always stop what he was doing, offer her a chair and ask what was the matter. I only asked once.

After that I recognised a pattern common in hypochondriacs, that of wanting to be centre of attention. In the course of the day, Myrtle seemed to attract physical complaints and accidents all around the school.

Once she was walking around a secondary P.E. lesson, in the quad, when a football collided with her head and she dropped her coffee cup which smashed on the tiled floor. She instantly screamed out and started weeping uncontrollably, much to the embarrassment of all present. The boy responsible for the out of control ball promised to replace her mug and was exceptionally apologetic. The P.E. lesson paused until Myrtle limped off back to the staffroom to compose herself. On another occasion she was almost knocked to the ground by a herd of boys stampeding round a corner. She was heard to wail "I can't stand this anymore! I am sick to death of these animals!"

Myrtle was definitely displaying signs of being unhinged. I decided to put some distance between me and her, but it wasn't so easy for Rupert who had to share the management role, with her as his deputy.

A music teacher, who went home to Ireland for the winter break, didn't return because the dust brought on severe bronchitis and she was advised by her doctor not to come back. We missed her: especially me because now I didn't have a specialist teacher for my music slot once a week and had to teach the subject myself. I streamed YouTube clips of sing-a-long songs, *London's burning*, *1-2-3* by Bruno Mars, *Dem bones*, and other child friendly ditties to fill in the time. It was the best I could come up with.

Even though the lifestyle of Kuwaiti children was inside focused and sedentary, all the children in school loved the P.E. lessons. I used this love of P.E. as a managerial tool. The threat of 'No P.E. for you this week,' sometimes worked, as the kids who were most badly behaved were the ones who most loved P.E. But I didn't usually see the threat through because I knew that the one hour, once a week lesson, was probably the only time the kids got to run around.

Statistics abound of how diet and lifestyle contribute to general poor health and diseases such as diabetes. Kuwait is ranked ninth in the world's most obese countries, so it is no surprise to learn that Kuwaitis have fully embraced the American style, fatty, sugary, salty, fast food culture. The various global chains and outlets are plentiful and obviously doing a roaring trade. It always made me smile to see the Platinum gym handily attached to the McDonald's drive through. Perhaps the idea is to work off the excess calories before you drive away; or to enjoy a fat reward for doing a hefty workout. Who knows? Kuwait is also on the list of the world's worst teeth for pretty much the same reasons.

There is a general disconnection in attitude toward health and fitness, which is reflected in what I saw around me. I noticed that in my neighbourhood men had gyms, hairdressers and massage parlours and women had hair, nail and beauty parlours, with no use for gyms. People spent a great deal of time in malls, eating and had the idea that doctors and dentists were there to 'fix' you, relieving the individual of any personal responsibility for their own health and well being: you simply make an appointment to get a pill or surgery.

This inside, inward looking lifestyle was, of course, a cultural thing and because, generally, it was not very pleasant to be outside. At school there was a shameful lack of outside space and all the P.E. lessons, for all year groups, were miraculously delivered in the quad.

Sports Day was fast approaching and my class were especially noisy and excited in the weeks running up to the event. There seemed to be the same level of buzz of anticipation as if it was the Olympics or some other high profile international games. A neighbouring playing field had been rented for the week and each year group was allotted their day for competing. The events were a sprint (about 100m), a long distance run (one lap round the pitch, about 500m), inter-class dodge-ball and inter-class football – boys and girls in separate teams. Rupert suggested we should involve the parents in a dish-dash: pure comedy genius.

The P.E. department organised the whole day, which meant that I just had to keep on top of potential violence between the children as they waited their turn to compete. On the whole though, everyone was quite well behaved. No-one wanted to be sent back to class for silent reading or extra maths - the threat I had used to manage the usual suspects.

I was mildly amused and quite saddened, in equal measure, by the general lack of physical fitness of the children. There were some that could run freely; move with the lightness of youth and chase a ball like a puppy. But there were others who seemed at odds with their own bodies; not quite sure how to use arms and legs, panting and puffing as they waddled across finish lines, or simply giving up and falling down at the side of the track.

At a qualifying football match, one of the popular boys in my class scored a goal. There were huge cheers and shouts as he zoomed around the pitch in a lap of honor the way Portuguese soccer star Christian Ronaldo does – arms outstretched behind like a jet fighter, mobbed by his team mates, then dropping to his knees in a classic champion's pose of glory, punching the air.

When we had all calmed down and were back in school, I asked if the football stars in our class planned to play for Kuwait. There were looks of misunderstanding so I framed the question another way.

"Why not play football for the Kuwait team?"

This idea seemed difficult for the children to process, then one of the girls said that there was no Kuwaiti football team. Surely there was. Everyone was football crazy here. But the children looked at each other and shrugged. They all had *Real Madrid* or *B.C.N.* logos on their school bags and lunch boxes. They all knew the names Neymar Junior, Messi and Ronaldo, of course, and argued who was the best player. These were the players that they had seen on television, scoring goals for teams in faraway lands. These were their heroes and football, it seemed, was something that happened outside Kuwait, in another country, in another world from theirs.

(Kuwait does have a national football team, but it has been banned from playing in international tournaments due to government interference and corruption allegations. The Kuwait soccer team last played in the FIFA world cup in 1982.)

I decided that I had to stay as healthy as possible because there was no way I wanted to go to a Kuwaiti medical centre. I was skeptical of the overall state of healthcare and whether, like other aspects of life here, it was just a glittery cardboard cutout of the real thing. The rumours of swine-flu, Dr Om Mohammed, Rupert's drama with blood tests and x-rays, and the Kuwaiti doctors story certainly made me conscious of keeping well, looking after myself and staying fit: I walked, I swam, I did yoga in my lounge.

Muscley P.E. Dave had joined one of the gyms close to our apartment building and was impressed by the facilities and equipment. For a while, non-muscley Tim, who looked like a pencil, went with him to train. He expressed concern that he was only working out to keep fit and that he didn't want to 'bulk up', as if muscles would suddenly appear on his puny frame.

Tessa, spurred on by some of our rather large-girthed colleagues and the fear of becoming one of them, made daily visits to the teachers' gym in the basement of the other building. Later, she would join a women's rugby team – in fact, the women's rugby team of Kuwait, as it turned out – and played away at tournaments in Dubai, Qatar and Abu Dhabi at weekends. Sandra and Rupert were similarly inspired to increase fitness and shed kilos.

The lack of places for social interaction; family and friends being far away; and expensive, and therefore out of reach, leisure activities, meant that there was quite a bit of spare time to be filled. At the end of a working day, there was that slippery slope to streaming movies, watching TV and eating junk in your air-conditioned lounge. Or you shifted your carcass into gear and got moving, seizing an opportunity for improved fitness and general health. It seemed in this place of extremes, you went one way or the other.

12

Swimming

There's poo in the pool. I found out at the morning briefing, that a leak in the sewage pipe had overflowed and caused a flood, that had been dripping a cloudy yellowy-brown liquid into the school pool, which was fanning out in a toxic plume. The area was necessarily sealed off and being dealt with. Shit. Literally.

I was traumatized.

The pool was my life line, my sanity, my mental re-set, a vital necessity to health and well-being. I communicated this on my non-negotiables, must-have, wish list to my recruiter, who assured me that there was a pool available for staff use.

"Great," I said, excited. "I accept the offer." And that was that.

Access to a pool had been close to the top of my wish list in accepting a teaching post. It was positioned equal to 'school, walking distance from home' and only just behind 'fully furnished flat and all utilities provided'. I had turned down a job in Qatar because there was no pool available for teacher use. There teachers were expected to join a gym with a pool. Nah. So when my recruiter phoned to say "Yes, there is definitely a pool," I remember thinking, "Wow, list of boxes ticked. I am all powerful, ha ha ha." (This last bit in the voice of an evil villain.)

Swimming is more than just exercise. It is meditation in motion. It is the best way I have found to de-stress the mind and body and to achieve a satisfying calm, all inside a half hour window. A swim marks the end of work and the beginning of me time. Apart from swim goggles and possibly a latex cap, no specialized gear is needed and, as with team or paired sports, there is no relying on other people to make things happen and therefore no-one to blame for your own laziness if you skip a day. After work, I simply find a pool, swim some laps. Job done. Then feel refreshed to enjoy a relaxed evening.

To say I was disappointed when I saw the 'pool available for teacher use' was an understatement. In my mind the 'pool available for teacher use' was rooftop, surrounded by loungers and potted palms with an expansive view of the city. The place to be for a sunset dip, idle chatter with colleagues; the water a nice tepid, possibly a little on the warm side for swimming laps, but hey, I could put up with that. Wrong, wrong and wrong again.

The 'pool available for teacher use' was in the basement of the old teachers' building, next to the gym, which stank of sweat and air-freshener, but mostly sweat. The pool was barely long enough to swim four strokes before hitting the other end and the temperature was surprisingly, a little above freezing. It remains a mystery how water could be this cold, when the water from the cold tap was almost as hot as water from the hot tap.

I braved the frigid, just-bigger-than-a-bath pool in the first few weeks of term, when the outside temperature made a plunge into freezing water appealing. I dashed in from the sweltering heat, changing as quick as possible and jumped in before my conscious mind could formulate argument. I could swim for around ten minutes before my head began to hurt and my teeth began to chatter. The blood in my system retracted from my extremities to save my vital organs as my core temperature plummeted. I was still shivering and goose-pimply all over as I stepped back out into the oven hot afternoon.

There was, however, another pool. This one was behind shutters in the school basement, but it was as yet unavailable for swims because it was awaiting its yearly clean and refill for the start of the new academic year, even though the first term was well under way. No-one seemed to know when this was going to happen. Most weeks I would stop by to look at the half metre of greenish stagnant water, willing it to be full and clear and swimming pool blue like a David Hockney painting.

It was November when I discovered that the school pool was fully functional. I was so super excited. The school pool was actually not bad; a standard 25m pool with lanes and a deep end. I could ignore the public toilet smell, the chipped tiles and the general could-do-with-a-do-up appearance. I could blank out the disrepair and grubbiness. It was a pool. The water was clear and best of all, warm.

I made a roster so men and women swam on different days. Mixed swims are *haram*. To be seen in ones bathers by someone of the opposite sex, who was not your husband/ wife or a close member of your immediate family, is a big no-no.

I looked forward to swim days and the feeling of moving through the water, focusing on breathing and not much else. By the time I walked home I felt at once light and heavy; light in my mood and having nothing in my head, and heavy in my tired limbs.

Now, after only a few happy weeks of swims, counted in laps not strokes, there was poo in the pool. And I was thrown into a deep depression. I considered going back to the basement pool, but the heat had gone from the day and the thought of plunging into the Arctic was unimaginable. One day, out of desperation, I did wander down to test the waters of the stinky basement pool. I put in my hand. 'See, it's not so bad,' I tried to convince myself. 'Are you completely mad!' was my reply.

After about a week of no swims, I decided to ask someone in the science department to test a sample of pool water for impurities. The sewerage leak that had closed the pool had been mended, the pool filter had been working the whole time, but I wanted to make sure I was not going to accidently contract e-coli or something worse if I took a dip. I bottled a sample of pool water and took it to the science lab for testing.

"I'll see what I can do," said Alfie, in secondary science, who was now flatting with P.E. Dave.

A week passed. I did my best to avoid the science staff and waited patiently, trying not to nag. Another week passed and I became

165

impatient. I tracked down Alfie and casually asked about the pool water.

"I wouldn't swim in it," he said without hesitation.

"Shit," I said. "Is it the shit? Is the water still contaminated?"

"No, not that."

"What then?"

"There is a toxic amount of chlorine, like way too much. It'll take your skin off."

I processed this information. Then went for a swim.

But surely if you want to swim, you can just go to a beach and swim in the sea. That's right. There are beaches in Kuwait. There is a whole big coast with sea and sand and even palm trees, date palms not coconut. This is true. There was even a beach at Al Kout, an easy twenty minute walk away from our front door, which became a regular destination for an evening stroll or a weekend stride.

But here was the catch, as a woman, you couldn't turn up for a swim, in a one-piece or bikini, without seriously drawing unwanted attention, and possible abuse, from passersby. Sexual segregation and the Muslim idea that showing your body in such a way is offensive and shameful meant that beach culture, in a western sense, is just not here. Even on a blistering hot day with the blue sea beckoning, you must stay covered up on a public beach.

The beach and corniche were popular with mostly immigrant families from the Indian subcontinent and South East Asia. They would picnic on rugs as the day dimmed, and wallow, fully covered up, in the slack, easy tide. Lights from the refinery and waiting tankers reflecting with the rising moon. Empty bottles rolling down to the water's edge and picnic packaging wafting to and fro in the evening waves, as the breeze brings the unmistakable aroma of the not too distant waste water treatment plant. I would kick off my sandals and walk ankle deep in the gently lapping waves, skillfully avoiding the half submerged broken glass, an ever-present danger.

Al Kout was close to home, but if you are a woman and if you want to swim, you need to go to a private beach. There are private, fenced-off beaches such as Egaila or Messina, where you pay an entrance fee, and there you can bathe in a bikini without fear of offending anyone or drawing too much attention to yourself. You will still be stared at, sure, but no-one will bother you.

If you are a man, however, you can swim happily and unhindered anywhere you wish. Cliff who liked to run in the evening would often end his exercise with a hearty half k swim in the waters off Al Kout beach. One particular occasion, while enjoying a dip, he came up for air close to what he assumed to be a half-submerged bag of rubbish. He swam away from the rubbish bag and made his way back to the beach. He thought nothing of it, until he saw the lights of ambulances and police vehicles close to where he had left his things on the sand. A crowd had gathered at the water's edge. Some people were gesticulating and chattering excitedly, others were quietly watching from a distance, craning their necks to see through gaps in the crowd. The focus of their attention was the 'bag of rubbish', which turned out to be the body of an old man that had been floating around in the Gulf for a few days. This put me right off beach swims.

Some weekends in the hot months, a taxi full of teachers would arrive with all they needed for a day out at the sea-side at Egaila beach, the nearest private beach. Afternoons were when the westerners would relax on towels with music turned up, slyly sipping home-made wine. There was a comforting nostalgia connected to these trips among the Brits in our group, who shared golden memories of U.K. family holidays at coastal resorts: of buckets and spades; of ice-cream and stripy deck chairs; of fish and chips eaten from a newspaper wrapping as the sun goes down. Blissful, lovely sunshine days that only exist in childhood memories.

The beach at Egaila was not much better or cleaner than Al Kout, but we could swim here and relax with bare skin exposed for an afternoon and feel a bit normal. For a beach-lover like me, I could over-look the windblown plastic bags caught in the chain-link fencing and the feral cats pooping in the sand around us, and the rusty barbed wire aggressively marking the boundary of the private beach area from the neighbouring property. At high tide, the water was deep enough so you could swim straight off the beach, but at low tide, you had to pick your way across jagged concrete, rocks and discarded tyres, out to a swimmable depth. But this was what we had. It was fine. I lay on my towel, feeling the warmth of the sand and sun on my skin, looking up into the bright blue sky, pretending I was somewhere else; somewhere pretty and natural and clean.

When the sun left the beach we did too. In the relative cool of the evening, that is when the Kuwaiti families would emerge and congregate around white plastic tables with barbeques and chip packets and shisha pipes: grandparents, aunties, uncles, cousins and a thousand million children on all the different kinds of wheels, zooming up and down the concrete walkway, squealing in delight. The still air would be filled with charcoal smoke and Arabic voices.

The alternative to paying for a day at a private beach was to become a member at one of the swanky five star hotels' leisure facilities. Annual membership at the Hilton or Radisson Blu or The Palms, which were all a short taxi ride away, was unfortunately, totally out of my budget. Although, we did enjoy a couple of 'taster' days: one time organised by the school and another time organised by me, at the Hilton in Mangaf, and The Palms in the up-market suburb of Salmiya.

I would never stay at these kinds of hotels. (Unless someone else was paying.) They are faceless, unwelcoming and stupidly expensive. They have an atmosphere that says... *our customers are demanding. Our customers have money to burn. Our customers can afford to pay five pounds for an orange juice poured from a litre carton which costs around one pound fifty, and they don't care. Our customers need at least three towels for the beach and pool area and they need someone to come and adjust their loungers. And then they will order food they will not eat. Our customers will stub out cigarettes on the floor even when an ashtray is right there. They will talk loudly into their cell phones, take selfies and laugh without any kind of humour behind it. They treat our staff with contempt. Our customers are oily and some have surgery to indicate there may be some abdominal muscles beneath a hefty layer of fat. Our customers don't swim in the pool; they bob at the edge wearing designer sunglasses, like toads in a pond.*

The Palms hotel had clearly missed the point of having a private beach. A temporary fence had been erected around the pool area with a gap in it if you did want to venture to the sea. Outside the fenced area between the fence and the sea, was a building site road, busy with diggers and bulldozers and other heavy machinery, for an extension project next door. While lying on a lounger under a shady date palm, I tried in vain to block out the noise from the builders, which was disturbing my relaxation. I put my book down, took off my sunglasses and stepped through the gap in the fence, careful to look both ways before continuing to the water's edge. Behind me was the temporary fence and building site, so I gazed out to sea and imagined I was at a beach in Goa. The water was silky and glassy smooth, and the noise was less intrusive the further out I swam.

I was enjoying flopping around, occasionally diving under and floating on my back, eyes closed, arms and legs starfished out in the bright Arabian sun. Bliss. When I stood up in the shallows I spotted a lazy fish just below the surface. When my eyes adjusted to the brightness of sun reflected on water, I realised that it was not a fish at all, but the unmistakable size and shape of a poo. I tried to block the reality of this image from my mind and although I did my best to pretend I hadn't seen it, I quickly had to leave the beach for a very thorough rinse off shower, followed by a dive into the toad pond. I didn't swim in the sea again after that.

170

At the Hilton there were three pools to choose from as well as the beach. It was lush. I swam in them all. Tessa, Sandra, Rupert and I had dragged ourselves out of the apartment after a messy night of home-made wine and dancing wildly to eighties hits. The Hilton taster day was a rare treat and a wonderful self-indulgent way to while away a hangover. When it became too chilly to be outside by the pool, we descended into the dimly lit spa where the hydrotherapy pool soothed my throbbing head. I reconsidered the membership fee. Maybe it was worth it after all.

13

Behind closed doors

Beside the mosque, outside the Ivory Tower, was a vast empty, yet-to-be-built-on space that we could view from the lounge window. Here, there were regular gatherings of men in dishdashas, who sat and chatted on hard-backed bench seats, which were set out in a large formal arrangement, around a square of rolled out Persian type rugs. There were canvas marquees and staff serving refreshments on trays. It was all lit with strings of festooned light bulbs. I was intrigued. What were they doing? What were they talking about? From my lounge window I tried to guess what was being said.

(Ahmed arrives at the marquee and steps onto the carpeted area where he is greeted by his friend Mohammed. They sit together on a hard backed bench with Omar, a mutual acquaintance.)

Ahmed: Hey Mohammed, thanks for inviting me. What's the occasion?

Mohammed: Oh y'know, just to get the boys together. Tea?

Ahmed: Sure. Thanks.

(Mohammed gestures to a servant to bring tea for him and his friends.)

Mohammed: So Ahmed, have you met Omar?

Ahmed: Yes, at that get together at the Grand Mosque last month.

Omar: Oh yes, that's right. How are you?

Ahmed: Good, good.

(Tea is served and there is a moment when the men sit in silence and drink their tea.)

Omar: I love your dishdasha. Is it new? It's so white.

Ahmed: Oh, this old thing!

Omar: Did you get it laundered or do you do it yourself at home?

Ahmed: I washed it myself, actually, with Persil. I'm so pleased you noticed. Yes, the whites do come out brilliantly. I only send mine to the laundry for a deep clean once a week... or if I spill my tea, haha.

(The men continue to drink tea and laugh quietly together as they watch more men arrive in white dishdashas.)

This is probably nothing like what is actually being said, although I do guarantee there would be at least one Mohammed, an Ahmed and maybe a couple of Omars present. This male only gathering was typical of an event that was strictly off limits for outsiders.

Society is closed off and not knowing anyone at all has been a bit of an issue for me living Kuwait. Usually on my travels, I can spot people who are my tribe i.e. folk I can have a laugh with, hang out, enjoy the company of, share a drink or a meal, go for a walk, see a band, get invited to parties, thus creating a social web of interactions and friendships, which give a sense of belonging and allow an individual to feel like a thread in the social fabric. Other than a few of my fellow teaching colleagues, and expats I have met randomly, I didn't meet anyone in Kuwait I would consider a friend.

The obvious barrier to creating social connections is language, of course. I don't speak Arabic and although English is generally everywhere, conversation is limited and people just don't seem interested in getting to know foreigners.

In a recent survey by *InterNations Expat Insider,* Kuwait was voted the least friendly country to be living as a foreigner. It was last on a list of sixty-four, and from my experience living here, I would agree. Saudi Arabia was second most unfriendly, while Oman, a neighbouring Arab nation, ranked in the top ten friendliest. Bahrain, also just down the road, came in at seventeen. (According to the survey, Myanmar is the friendliest, followed by Mexico and Portugal, in case you were wondering.)

This unfriendliness stems from a perception of cultural superiority and pride in being a descendant from one of the original tribes of Kuwait. The children at school also displayed a sense of superiority to the non-Kuwaiti children in school. Rupert, who as head of primary, dealt with a lot of violence and bad behaviour, which arose from racial issues and children saying 'bad' words to each other. He remembers one incident involving two boys who were apprehended in a year five class and sent to his office.

Rupert: So, you're telling me that you hit Mohammed because he said a bad word to you.

Ahmed: Yes mister. He say very bad word for me.

Rupert: Mohammed. What did you say to Ahmed?

Mohammed: I say that he is Iraqi.

Rupert: And that's why you hit him?

Apparently, to call someone Iraqi is a huge insult, meaning that the person in question is very stupid.

I noticed other racial superiority in class, especially among the boys. One child was being bullied because he was from Armenia and another boy was teased to tears because he was told that he was not a pure Kuwaiti, therefore inferior and not allowed to join in with a game. But being a pure Kuwaiti had its down side as the obvious traits of inbreeding showed in the children lined up at assembly.

At school I had a solid crew of fellow teaching staff to rely on for laughs and camaraderie, but outside of the school it was pretty tricky to be in a situation where friendships happen, as regular environments of social interaction are not here. I get the very strong feeling that everything is happening behind closed doors, in private, invite only, no-one else allowed, especially nosy white female immigrants who are simply just not welcome.

Early on in the year, I did make an effort to meet some people outside school and went to a party, organised by a social network group that organises parties. The venue was uptown near the Sheraton in Kuwait City. There were a few of us newbies who, like me were thinking, 'Haha. Party. Everything is going to be alright now'.

The ticket was kind of pricey, considering it was just a party with DJs and not a festival with live music, but hey, I was in, it was a party and I was going to meet some fun people. We were going to laugh and dance and maybe drink a little cheeky alcohol.

The theme was *Around the World* and was apparently a big night on the expat social calendar. Guests were encouraged to dress in an outfit which reflects their country – could be national dress, colours of the flag, or.....well, you get it. The outline was loose and open to broad interpretation.

Luckily for me and Tessa, we manage to get a ride in a car with a Spanish couple; she, a P.E. teacher at school, he, well I still don't really know, something to do with fertility clinics. They had been to the event the previous year and were enthusiastic about going again. They had even acquired some bootleg date wine, which was more like a thick, sticky liqueur than a wine, but I was not about to complain. I accepted with due grace and gratitude, climbed into the back seat and we were away.

We parked behind an apartment building somewhere uptown in the labyrinth of streets. Looking up I could see that all the windows on every floor were dark except the eighth floor, which was pulsing with a coloured light show and there was a distant thud of a base line in the otherwise still and quiet evening.

176

Parties and consumption of alcohol are technically forbidden, so I'm looking up at the venue thinking about the potential consequences to my soon-to-be actions. But I don't really have time to weigh up my options because my car buddies have already disappeared into the building and have called the lift. Right then. I follow.

Two enormous bouncers greet us as we step out of the lift and check our tickets, then wordlessly indicate the direction we should go. They look exactly the way bouncers are supposed to, straight out of the movies; huge, imposing, arm muscles bulging through suit jacket, black t-shirt, big gold chain on a massive chest, no hair, big neck, impassive expression. There were a few of these giants stationed throughout the apartment, so I guessed security was where the bulk of the ticket revenue was spent.

Through a double door and the music is loud, hard, banging techno. Groups of costumed people stand in groups holding onto plastic cups, chatting politely. There is a row of tables against one wall with different kinds of fizzy drinks, some ice in a bucket, plastic disposable cups and bags of crisps laid out like a child's birthday party.

The floor is white marble inset with glass panels, which illuminate white decorative pebbles beneath. There are a few chairs and low tables hugging the interior walls, but the exterior wall is a huge semi-circular window with a sweeping view over the city lights.

I have my plastic cup with date wine and a little ice from the beverage table and I'm feeling quite good. The music is not my cup of tea, but it's danceable, and I'm out and there are people not from school to meet, although it seems like there are a lot of teacher-types in the room. As more people arrive, the room fills with mostly white western expats. There are some other nationalities and Kuwaitis present who remain aloof and unimpressed. They make no effort to mingle.

I chat for a bit with two Peruvian men from the embassy, who are unmistakable in wooly hats and ponchos. There are a couple of Cleopatras, some Hawaiian style hula girls in raffia skirts and colourful leis. There are a lot of rugby and football shirts from various nations, a Buddhist monk and an Indian sa'dhu complete with prayer beads and a chanting stick. Some people had gone to a great deal of effort with their presentation and attention to detail, which always inspires admiration in me, as someone who doesn't really bother with dress ups. I wore a t-shirt I bought in Chiapas, Mexico, which had a slogan of the Zapatista rebellion printed on it; a lame effort in comparison.

"Hey, I like your t-shirt," said one of the Peruvians. "You don't look Mexican."

"I'm not."

As the evening progressed, I observed the crowd; danced more, talked less. Then the pizza arrived, which made everything even more like a child's birthday. The white marble floor was fast becoming as slippery as an ice-rink and at regular intervals girls in heels would slide over in a whoosh, pulling down anyone who happened to be close by, inevitably causing more drinks to be spilled, increasing the general slipperiness of the floor. And so it continued with the flailing of arms and legs, and shrieks of surprise cutting through the thumping music. The DJs, who were also the party organisers, annoyingly kept stopping tracks part way through to sound an air-horn and shout into the mic "Make some noise!" This practice should be used sparingly and is only really acceptable when a party has reached its peak and at no other time. On reflection I believe the incessant air-horn use was a flimsy distraction to mask the dismal mixing skills on the decks.

Things were quickly getting messy. There was some outrageous drunken flirtation and jealous sulking, some mad dancing, and tuneless sing-a-longs to cheesy dance anthems. Around the edges of the dance floor sat the non-expats, highly polished, bored looking, sunglasses wearing and dripping in gold jewellery, viewing the revelry with cool detachment. It was late and I was not at all upset when I got the nod that my ride was ready to leave.

I didn't really bother with going out after that. In February there was a Valentine's Ball organised by the same organisers. Some of my colleagues bought outfits and got their nails done, thinking it might be good, but it was at the same venue and I just had a sneaking feeling that it was going to be a repeat of the *Round the World* party. I waved them off like Cinderella, but without the feeling of missing out. I knew what the night was going to be like and by all accounts, my suspicions were correct.

Meeting people in Kuwait was not easy. As I've mentioned elsewhere in this book, there are a lack of public spaces and going-out places to meet people, as you would in other urban areas around the world. Plus there is a rigid structure to the societal status of women.

At school the gender gap is astonishing for someone brought up with sexual equality as a cultural ideal to strive for. I am pedantic in avoiding gender stereotypes. I have had to bite my lip a number of times at school, when I noticed girls being praised for being pretty, sitting quietly aside, while boys were pushed to play sport and take the lead. All the visual cues clearly learned from Disney because on dress-up days, the girls arrive all dolled up as princesses complete with painted nails, immaculately coiffed hair and elaborate make-up, and the boys wear their choice of super hero, football star or pirate.

Meeting women in a social setting outside school is almost impossible. Kuwaiti women are still regarded as property of men – someone's daughter to someone's wife to someone's mother. They are usually not present publicly without an entourage of family members and children. Most still dress from top to toe in black abaya, they appear to be reserved and shy. So when Sandra was invited to a wedding she jumped at the chance to have a look inside this very closed female culture.

Sandra was invited as the guest of Jane, from Learning Support at school, who had tutored someone from the family of the bride. Jane and her partner lived in an apartment in Fintas, one of the neighbouring suburbs to Mangaf. They owned a car, so she volunteered to drive to the wedding, which was an address in Salwa, an

180

up market suburb close to the city centre. The invitation stated a 10 p.m. start.

Although the pair left in plenty of time for the journey up town, they became disorientated by the convoluted road system of Salwa, and after a while of driving round trying to find the venue, Sandra sent a text to the friend asking for more information, a land mark or something to look out for.

The reply came back.

"Yes Salwa is vry big ;)"

Sandra acknowledged this response, then repeated that they still couldn't find the wedding venue and needed help.

"Come now?" was the reply.

Eventually, and by sheer chance, after driving round and round, they found the place but missed the ceremony. The bride had already left with the groom and the male guests had moved on to the male only part of the evening. The female guests remained in the lavishly decorated hall of the events centre. They chatted and laughed together wearing traditional black hijabs and abayas. Then something quite surprising happened. The older women stayed seated around the raised staging area while the younger women jumped up on the stage, whipped off their abayas, revealing brightly coloured western style party dresses. They yelled a high pitched wail typical at Arabic celebrations, and strutted up and down the catwalk suggestively in a kind of potential daughter-in-law dance off for the seated, potential mother-in-laws.

Under the traditional outer-wear, the women had spared no expense in presentation. They had all obviously spent a great deal of time and dinar at salons for nails and hair. Their dresses were showy, revealing cleavage, upper arm and thigh, and all the young women seemed to have skin that was glittery pinkish-white, probably in the same way that people with white skin get a spray tan for a special occasion.

Sandra and Jane watched this extraordinary parade, extended greetings to their hostess and then left the family and friends to continue the celebrations. They sensed that they had been invited as a novelty or status symbol for the bride. As if some westerners at your wedding elevated the family's social esteem, 'Ah yes, these are some white girls we know, impressive huh?' Or maybe some expats just served as further decoration for the wedding venue.

My world became quite small with the lack of social interaction, so it was a breath of fresh air to meet Marie one weekend. Marie was from mid-West America and was here teaching adults at the Ministry of Defense base in the desert, outside Kuwait City. She is a self-confessed hippy and had a gig teaching yoga a couple of evenings a week at the Hilton. She had been in Kuwait a year already and she was looking forward to moving on somewhere else. "Maybe somewhere East of here, with a bit more soul."

The bus from the old teachers' building was scheduled to leave each Saturday at 10a.m. and return from *The Avenues* mall at 1p.m. It was free for the MoD teachers, and other teachers were welcome to tag along if there was room. I had no real reason to go to *The Avenues*. I generally don't enjoy malls: they remind me of airports, a kind of no-man's-land of fluorescent light, air-con and bubblegum music. But the bus was free and it was a trip out, somewhere.

Most of the other seats on the bus were occupied by MoD employees - all American and all men: the kind of men who wore their cell phones in a holster like a gun, and pulled their white sports socks up around their calves. They wore Hawaiian shirts tucked into chino knee-length shorts and sat upright, chewing gum and looking out of the window, through wrap-around shades.

Marie, by contrast, was the opposite of the male staff. She was defiantly feminine, wearing her hair down and loose, with a colourful t-shirt, flared jeans and leather sandals. We were instant friends and talked non-stop about everything, all the way to the mall. It was so lovely to meet someone of my tribe. We swapped numbers and stayed in touch. Marie and I would meet up some afternoons and stride briskly to Al Kout beach, chat, laugh, drink carrot juice and share work stories.

"I have this group of students," she tells me. "They're all, you know, young and think they're in *Top Gun* or something. Anyway, to get some kind of conversation going, I ask them questions, like 'What do you think about the American presence here in your country? How do you feel about it?' This one student raises his hand and says 'Well, if the Americans left, we wouldn't know what to do. They tell us what to do and we do it.' These are professional, highly paid personnel, remember!"

We laugh loud and hard while sitting on a bench, looking at the tankers queuing up at the refinery wharf.

Marie takes another sip of carrot juice.

"Then, another time, we get around to talking about wars, and I ask them what they know about the Second World War. Touchy subject, I know, but hey. And do you know what one of them said? He said it was a shame what happened to the Jews. I thought he meant that he felt sorry about what happened, the death camps and all. But no, that's not what he meant. He meant it was a shame that Hitler didn't kill them all."

We didn't laugh at this one and sat silently for some time.

Marie gave me an insight into another side of Kuwait, outside the hamster-wheel of my life, which was spiraling in on itself. She moved on and out before I did and I missed her hippy presence.

At school, Tessa had met Zara, a classroom assistant from Early Years. Zara was from Lebanon and was living in Kuwait with her husband and two young daughters.

"I see you, habibi, and I think, yani, you are for me. Your eyes and your hair, yani. And I think I am for you too."

At first, Tessa didn't mind the regular visits to her classroom. Zara was affable and chatty, and Tessa was open to making social contacts, so they exchanged numbers and arranged a night out with some of Zara friends.

"I will come for you, yani. You will see something of life, habibi. My friends they speak English, yani. I will show you."

Zara was early. Tessa had just stepped out of the shower, when the beep beep came through on her mobile, that Zara was five minutes away.

"Shit," said Tessa simultaneously blow-drying her hair and pulling on jeans.

In the car, Zara was crying, streaking her make-up in black lines down her face. Her two young daughters sat on the back seat with a voiceless maid. Her husband was driving. Tessa climbed into the back seat with the maid and the children.

"We have to take them to my sister's house and my father's house. My sister she say she cannot have the two girls, yani, so I ask my father and he said for me yes it's ok and now he says no. He always does this. He makes it hard for me, yani. He does nothing for me. He hates me! WALLAH!"

Zara's husband waited for his wife's wailing to subside before introducing himself. Tessa smiled and nodded back, then she introduced herself to the maid, who continued staring directly ahead.

The two girls looked at Tessa, then looked away. The car pulled out into the traffic.

Zara's sister was waiting in a car, at a vacant lot, in a suburb, about twenty minutes away. The journey was peppered with emotional outbursts from Zara, in Arabic, and periodic beeps from her mobile phone. Zara's father's house was in another suburb on the way to *Arabella's* mall, which was the meeting place for the evening.

Arabella's is in Hawally, usually around a thirty minute drive from Mangaf, but with all the driving around and dropping off dramas, Tessa had been in the car a good hour and a half before they eventually arrived at the mall. Zara's friends were waiting at a restaurant, seated at an outside table on the thoroughfare. This, she learned, was a premium location at the mall, as it allowed the restaurant guests to see, as well as to be seen. Tessa was introduced to the women before pulling up a chair and sitting next to Zara.

Zara's friends were poised, polished, perfumed and unsmiling. Their body language suggested that Zara was the outsider and Tessa was Zara's newly acquired pet. They spoke together in Arabic, occasionally glancing over at Tessa in her Top Shop t-shirt, black jeans and Converse All-Star lace-ups.

"You are married?" asked one of the women.

"No," replied Tessa and that was the end of the conversation in English. The Kuwaiti women were clearly disinterested in this western woman who couldn't even attract a husband, and no wonder, when you saw how she was dressed!

The waiter brought out some menus, which were waved away. Then, without warning the group of ladies stood up and stalked off.

"We go to another place," said Zara and they hurried to keep up.

Arabella's is the place to be on a Friday night for the young and trendy in Kuwait City. Herds of women strut around in high heeled shoes and tight-fitting clothes, while herds of men watch from restaurant tables, drinking tea and smoking shisha. There are still women that wear more traditional dress of black abayas and hijabs, but for the sexually eligible, Friday night at *Arabella's* is the Kuwaiti equivalent of 'going clubbing'.

Tessa and the group of Zara's friends took a detour to the ladies' for a make-up touch up. Inside the public convenience, crowds of young women jostle for position at the mirror - spraying perfume, back-combing hair, re-applying lip gloss, sparkly eye-shadow and mascara. They bend forward to re-arrange cleavages and plump up breasts, pouting and posing like a night-club at two in the morning. Slightly overwhelmed by this frenzied activity, overcome with the mist of various odors and the cacophony of clucking, Tessa carefully backed out of the ladies' room, miming to Zara that she would be waiting outside.

After that evening, Zara assumed that she and Tessa were best friends forever and would ambush her at any time, during the school day.

"Habibi, you will come to Egypt with me and my children and my husband," she insisted, breathlessly, with a wide-eyed sense of urgency.

"I will find you a husband, yani. You must have babies. Look at you, yani. Your eyes and your hair!" as she made large gestures with her hands of a baby being born.

This liaison with Zara became intense and bizarre. Her attentions tipped from the label of 'friend' to 'stalker' in a matter of minutes. Tessa found she was spending her day at school trying to avoid running into Zara and when she did, she sought company so they would never be on their own. Things had got out of hand with this sad and deranged woman and Tessa felt inept to deal with it. She ignored the texts, calls and invitations, which beep-beeped at evenings and weekends. Hiding and avoidance was taking its toll and Tessa became exhausted by Zara's continual harassment. After a while of distancing herself, the torrent of contact from Zara lessened and Tessa began to relax, sensing that Zara had finally got the hint. But one day in her class, as she waved goodbye to the last child, Zara cornered her.

"Habibi, I have a groom for you. He sees your picture. He want you. What is your answer?"

14

Food

I must have been gazing middle-distance, as the scene with the sexy fireman drifted into my head, when our year leader, Frances bounced me back down to earth.

"And, this week we have Pink Day."

I tried not to look startled, noting down the information on the relevant pages of my diary.

"Well, if there are no questions, we're done. Enjoy your week."

The next day Joanne reminded the school at flag ceremony, "Don't forget that this Tuesday is Pink Day!"

There were simultaneous murmurs of dread from teachers, who had already experienced the phenomenon, and whoops of glee from the children.

I became nervous.

Joanne continued brightly and paced up and down, like a circus ringmaster, as she spoke into the microphone.

"Bring cake. Bring buns! Lots of buns! Bring biscuits and cake. I want cake. Bring me cake! You might decide to buy cakes from a shop or you might decide to bake some yourself. But don't forget – wash your hands". This last piece of advice was delivered in a low somber tone. "Thank you teachers. Thank you students."

Pink Day is a fundraiser for cancer awareness, and the search for a possible cure. Pretty serious and thought provoking? Not so here. Judging by the reaction of the children, Pink Day seemed to have the weight and sobriety of a Disney parade.

Back in the classroom, I asked the children what Pink Day was all about to find out what they knew.

"What is Pink Day?" I asked.

"It's when we bring cake and everything is pink!" one girl blurted out without raising her hand.

Then other voices chimed in loudly, relating details of the pleasures of Pink Day in a tumult of squeals and yelps.

"We wear pink and eat pink. There's pink everywhere!"

"Yes," I say, after quieting the excitement, "but why?"

"So we can bring cake and it's pink."

Having assessed that the children didn't have a clue, I clearly explained about cancer being a terrible disease and the need for research, so that a cure could be discovered and lives could be saved. Pink Day was a way of raising money and awareness of the disease, and all the money collected from people who paid one KD to swap their school uniform for pink clothes for the day, and from the sale of cakes, would go towards this worthy cause. I could see from the blank expressions that my message was not getting through. The only words that activated any recognition were 'pink' and 'cake'. Oh well, I tried.

Tuesday, as expected, started with a buzz. Girls arrived decked out fully in pink, from head to foot. Boys wore superhero and soccer team outfits. They brought bags and boxes of cakes and biscuits, which began to pile up in one corner of the classroom, then across tables and shelving. Some of the children had made 'Happy Pink Day' greetings cards for each other, as if this was a celebration of pink cake. It all had precious little to do with the awareness of a life threatening medical condition.

The lessons I had planned for that day went out of the window, as midway through maths, a maid arrived with even more bags of cake that had been dropped off by well-wishing parents. The bags were emblazoned with logos in Arabic and English from the numerous specialty cake shops prevalent on every street – *Chateaux de Gateaux, House of Chocolate, Finesse - for the finest cakes and sweets.* The cakes were lavish in their presentation of cellophane and ribbons; cupcakes with pink fondant swirls, glittering with icing and sugar; birthday sized cakes expertly decorated with flowers and hearts. There were boxes of pink iced doughnuts; individually wrapped chocolates in pink shiny paper and one very large cake even had the inscription "Happy Pink Day!" in pink, curly lettering and a sugar transfer of Sleeping Beauty. My teeth ached just looking at it all.

The fizziness of the classroom bubbled until break time when I explained how we were going to go about the class cake sale - sensibly and in a controlled manner.

Mohammed had his hand up the whole time I was speaking.

"Yes Mohammed."

"Can I eat my cake?"

"Of course, but you have to pay for it."

"Why? I bring."

"Because you brought the cake to sell so the money goes to help people with cancer," I explained.

"I don't want to buy. I bring. I eat."

"Fine."

With the help of two sensible girls, I arranged some of the swag of goodies, choosing the items which didn't need cutting and would possibly cause the least amount of mess. The children lined up, made their choice of just two items, paid their money to the two sensible girls, then went to sit down at their tables.

Of course I joined in and bit into a sickly sweet cup cake, which didn't taste of anything except sugar, so I threw it away.

I soon noticed that the serviettes, which were to be used as plates and to wipe sticky fingers, were not quite up to the task. Half eaten cup cakes and doughnuts lay abandoned on desks and other classroom surfaces. Items of sweet, sugary pinkness littered the floor. The call to place uneaten bits carefully in the rubbish bin, had resulted in a loose pile of messiness on the floor around the bin. I shut down the make-shift cake sale shop and ordered a straight quiet line, so the children could burn off some sugar fueled energy in the quad.

After what seemed a long time of getting some form of calm and quiet, I reminded my class to wash their hands before the end of break and then in a very loud voice said, "Please do not touch anything!"I could already see smears of pink icing on the tiled wall outside the classroom and some large blobs were trailing down to ground level. By the time we got to the quad the quiet, straight line was destroyed, as the children pushed and collided with each other to get down the stairs and start tearing round the shared space, crazed on their sugary overload.

Back in the classroom, I made an attempt to manage the left-overs, which were plentiful. I shoveled doughnuts back into boxes and covered the still complete cup cakes with cellophane, and then piled it all back in the bags and boxes they had arrived in. There was still a whole heap which had not even been opened. Anything that looked less than untouched was binned. I cleaned the stickiness from the cash and placed it in an envelope.

The remainder of the day ended up being a case of putting out fires. The children weren't able to do anything which required focus or concentration. The noise level steadily rose until it seemed like everyone was yelling, including me, and I had to send children for time out, left and right. Bad words were said 'for me' and 'for my mother' and erasers and pencils, which should have been used for writing, were now missiles.

The end of the day did not come soon enough.

When the last child had been collected, I flopped down onto my chair and surveyed the classroom. It was as if someone had broken in and caused willful damage with pink food. I did my best to clean up and asked for advice on what to do with the still unopened bags of cake and biscuits.

Our esteemed leader's idea? "We're going to do it all again tomorrow."

Pink Day was a successful fundraiser. A lot of money was collected from the classroom cake sales and children who paid for the privilege of wearing pink clothing or whatever, instead of school uniform for the day. But I kept thinking was it really an appropriate way to give to a worthy cause? What did it teach the children about the reality of cancer? How was the cash going to be used? What about health and diet in general? What about the element of waste?

The left-over cakes from the second day of the sale were given to the maids and, sad to say, most of the pinkness ended up in the skip, across the road at the back of the school. Each day a man would climb into the school skip in the searing temperatures, to forage for useful items such as cans or cardboard. Today he would find pink cake.

Food was a major issue at school. Tessa had been in a pitched battle from day one, trying to get the children to eat less processed food and more fresh fruit and veges. And to educate the parents in monitoring the content of lunchboxes. The problem was that the parents didn't put the lunches together. This task was done by the family's maid, who would place the easy to open packets of biscuits, crisps, sweets and chocolate, neatly with boxes of juice or chocolate milk, in a plastic lunch box for each child, each day.

At school, there was a snack shop, which stocked crisps, chocolate bars, sandwiches made with sweet white bread, pizza slices, popcorn and cartons of sugary fruit juice. It was misleadingly called *The Healthy Food Shop*.

The diet and general eating habits of the children, went some way to explain the fizzy, out-of-control nature of the final third of the day, after lunch. The children would eat their highly processed, sugary, salty snacks and buy more sugary, salty snacks from the snack shop, and be back in class just in time for the chemical processes of food additives to kick in, and turn their brains to mush. To try and teach anything in the after lunch slot was almost impossible, so I filled that time with shared reading or creative group work, and tried to stay on top of the rising noise levels, as I counted down to the end of the day.

As a subconscious reaction to what I saw the children eat, I sought solace in other food. I only had to look at a doughnut for my teeth to start aching and cake of any sort was highly unappealing. The biggest surprise, and something that I could not have even imagined, was I went off chocolate. It seemed that the exposure to sugary, fatty substances was like a virus I didn't want to catch. My consciousness became highly tuned to 'bad' food and it was everywhere at school.

Kuwaitis love to eat. Eating out is the most popular past time the whole family can enjoy. The evidence is clear from the number of eateries available at shopping malls and along the beach side roads, which always look busy. There are also, seemingly endless café and restaurant projects in various stages of construction, with names such as *The Village*, *Levels* or *The Lakes*. These are eating destinations, malls without the shops, where you will find all different kinds of global chain food outlets, grouped together in one spot with ample parking close by.

Food was something I had not really considered in any depth before. I knew roughly what a body needed to function – protein, minerals, blah, blah, blah, but now, since living in Kuwait, each meal was not merely a pit stop to refuel, but, at the risk of sounding cosmic, a sensual, pleasurable moment of taking in all the goodness for my whole entire being.

The local fruit and vegetable shop, *Day Fresh*, was on the way home from school and I stopped by most days to indulge in sun-ripened, un-sweetened, off-the-tree, out-of-the-ground, fragrant, unpackaged, locally grown produce. I discovered a new appreciation for flavours and colours. As my life spiraled inward on itself, becoming smaller and smaller, so the littlest of things, such as things I ate, grew large and important.

I explored the wonders of dates: there was a variety for my every culinary need. There were dates like a fancy wrapped caramel in a presentation box that was an indulgent sweet treat. I discovered sesame coated dates that, although were a bit disappointing to eat by themselves, were ideal cooked in porridge. There were dates that I would chop and de-stone for an addition to muesli, and dates I could just devour from their sticky wrapper. I researched the dietary properties of dates and was happy to learn we should all be eating more.

I've never been into cooking, and as it turned out, neither had Tessa, so our brand new gas oven stayed off. I became a whizz with the microwave and could turn out an infinite variety of dishes, from poached eggs and salmon on mashed garlic potatoes and spinach, my favourite brunch, to sushi, tom-yum soup and curry laksa. I delighted in deliciousness of combinations for salads; experimenting with rice, pasta, chickpeas and lentils. I was a master at creating a colourful, symphony of flavours in a bowl.

"I've found the perfect mango!" was not an unusual thing to hear at the Ivory Tower. Tessa and I would often relish our fruit and vegetable purchases, congratulating each other on choice of avocado or melon, with applause and grins. There was an overwhelming sense of satisfaction at picking out the best looking produce and taking it home like a prize.

My life had become very small.

Occasionally, I would go to the Indian restaurant, a block away from our flat. 'Restaurant' is perhaps too fancy a word for this eating establishment, even though the word is clearly printed on the signage above the door. It is, like all the other Indian restaurants in our area, small and basic; a no frills eatery with fluorescent lighting and utilitarian tables and chairs. This is not a place of decor or atmosphere. The TV is permanently on, tuned to a Hindi channel. This is a place where hungry workers get sustenance in order to continue working. The menu is on the wall.

I always go in with an open mind and the idea, that maybe I might try something new from the menu, but the masala dosa always wins out. Its tasty spiced potatoes stuffed into the rice pancake, generously spills over the sides of the metal plate, accompanied by aromatic chilly and coconut sauces. It was what I craved after a few glasses of home-made wine at the end of the working week. I would drunkenly waddle down to the restaurant and place my order in my 'I'm-not-the-slightest-bit-drunk' voice, ignoring the stares of boiler-suited immigrant workers hunched over their curry and rice.

One day, Dave popped round and presented Tessa and I with a cupcake. He had been given some from an adoring student at school. The sponge was a dark brown and the icing, a pretty violet, which was encrusted with sugar coated sweets. The cupcake was carefully placed in an elaborate, plastic see-through box, tied with a decorative ribbon the same colour as the purple icing. It had the look of something an evil step-mother would give to a princess in order to cast a devilish spell, or simply to poison causing a long, slow painful death. We extended our thanks, then left the cupcake isolated on the disused oven top.

It became a fixture of the kitchen and a science experiment. Over the following months, I observed the cupcake every day and noticed that nothing happened. The icing was as perfect as the day the cake was brought into our lives. The sponge had maintained its form, the icing was intact. In fact, apart from the colour fading from the decorative purple ribbon, there seemed to be absolutely no deterioration at all.

Alarmingly, the cupcake, which was supposed to be food and therefore organic matter, was showing no signs of decomposing. It sat smugly on its square of gold cardboard inside its mini display cabinet, immortal as the pharaohs of Egypt.

15

Fun

Thankfully, only two weeks in at the start of the year was *Eid*, 'festival of sacrifice'- a pretty big deal in the Arab world. It is a holiday time of feasting that coincided with the pilgrimage to Mecca known as *Hajj*.

At school, the Arabic staff put on a show to enlighten and entertain: a re-enactment of what to expect in Mecca. The Arabic and Islamic male teachers dressed in what looked like white towels and table-cloths, wrapped around the waist then over one shoulder. A handful of children from each class were chosen to perform as well. The boys were similarly dressed in white, while the girls were dressed in black abaya with their heads covered. Boys and girls stood in groups of black and white, separately.

The classes were called down in year groups and were seated on the floor, around the outside perimeter of the quad, to watch. A child-sized, yellow, paper-mache mountain on wheels was placed in one corner along with a life-sized toy sheep, and a replica of the *Kaaba*, also on wheels, was placed in the middle. The Kaaba, meaning cube, is the black monument in the grand mosque at Mecca, which is central to Islamic beliefs. There was a large foam-board poster of Arabic writing, propped up on a chair by the painted black box of the imitation Kaaba.

A narrator told everyone what was happening loudly in Arabic, into a mic.

First of all, two boys with toy daggers took a bottle of ketchup over to the paper-mache mountain and graphically acted out a slaughtering of the toy sheep. They were enthusiastically cheered on by their friends in the audience. Then the mic was handed over to one of the men dressed in white, as he led a chant and a procession of children round the Kaaba.

While the procession was in full swing the two boys who had acted out the sacrifice, were now using their daggers in a theatrical sword fight. I'm not sure if this was part of the action, or just that the boys, having done their bit, were now bored and were amusing themselves.

The chanting and processing continued around the Kaaba, which at regular intervals caused wafts of moving air strong enough to dislodge the foam-board poster from its propped up position on the chair. Every time it fell to the floor a female member of the Arabic staff would rush forward to replace it, only to watch it waft down again moments later.

The procession slowly exited, still chanting, and the boys with the daggers left their corner with the bottle of ketchup: the purpose of which remained a mystery. Whether the ketchup was present as an accompaniment to the pretend slaughtered sheep, or to represent the blood of the dead animal, or for some other reason, I will never know. The sheep now lay on its side beside the paper-mache mountain. The mic was handed back to the narrator who said something to wrap it all up. Whatever was said invited uproarious applause and cheers, which was enough to dislodge the poster for the final time.

Everyone travels at Eid. Flights were expensive and booked out, so I saw this as a good opportunity to explore Kuwait City with my tourist hat on, and have some fun. I looked online to see what was on offer and make a loose plan for the week's entertainment. I found a promo video showing Arab stallions and desert fortresses; lush green golf courses with decorative fountains; gardens and water features; camel racing and luxurious palaces; spectacular skylines and futuristic architecture. "Gosh," I thought, "where are these places?"

Outside my window was the opposite of this promo vid, a view of dusty beige ugliness. I was keen to find this other Kuwait: the good looking one.

I typed into my laptop 'top 10 things to do in Kuwait City', and found the following:-

1. Kuwait Towers
2. The Avenues – shopping mall
3. The Aquarium and Scientific Centre
4. Souk Mubarakia
5. Sief Palace
6. Diving and snorkeling – Qaruh Island
7. The Grand Mosque
8. House of Mirrors
9. The National Museum
10. Failaka Island

The Kuwait Towers, the Souk, The Avenues and the Grand Mosque were already ticked. We had been treated to a look-around bus trip by the school. The Aquarium and Scientific Centre would probably be a school trip destination, ditto the National Museum. Snorkeling at Qaruh Island would probably have been a go, but the short film clip which showed some brownish coral and one harassed blue fish, didn't look promising. Failaka Island, which was an historic strategic outpost since before the time of Alexander the Great, was going to be an expensive mission and, judging by photos, not a particularly attractive place to relax – a dusty beach, no palm trees and grim remnants of the war in the form of barbed wire and bullet-holed concrete buildings.

Later in the year, Helen did get it together for a day trip to Failaka Island. She found the sailing schedule, took a forty-five minute taxi ride to the ferry terminal, queued up, paid the fare, boarded the vessel, took her seat. She viewed the grey, blustery weather through the window as the ferry heaved itself out to the gulf. Helen gripped the arm-rest as the ferry started to lurch in all directions. After an hour or so, the ferry slowed in approach to a wharf. Helen noticed how similar the ferry terminal was at Failaka Island to the one she had left behind at Kuwait City. The ferry docked and all the passengers disembarked. It turned out that the ferry had indeed returned to its point of departure due to bad weather. There was no announcement or apology although, on enquiry, Helen was told her ticket would be valid if presented for any later sailings. I don't think she bothered.

This left the Sief Palace, which quite frankly just looked boring, and the intriguing House of Mirrors.

An online blurb describes it thus…

In the suburbs of Qadisiya you will find a miniature museum where every detail is scrupulously made of thousand broken mirrors. The widow of well-known artist in Kuwait Khalifa al Quattan, took her idea after decorating some furniture pieces. Lidia al-Qattan adorned an entire house with heroic scenes called Room of the Universe (bedroom), Basin of the Sharks (hallway) etc.

All the mirror montages were made from 77 tons of mirror and 102 tons of white cement. If you decide to visit this extraordinary piece of art just don't forget to bring a small present.

I read reviews which were mostly positive and so I proposed a visit to Helen, who was keen, and Sandra and Rupert. Tessa had flown out to visit a friend in Oman.

"It looks mental. We should go," said Rupert with enthusiasm.

I phoned and made an appointment as directed, then we piled into a taxi and took off up town. The house was indeed in a suburban street and as we entered the courtyard, Lidia was there to greet us. She was short and petite and wore a black ankle-length dress in chiffony layers.

"Welcome, welcome," she smiled welcomingly arms outstretched welcoming us in.

We were ushered passed another group of visitors who were occupying a reception room just inside the front door, and into a room off the hallway. It was a wonder of mirror mosaic depicting planets, shooting stars, moons and suns. We were asked to wait and relax on the built-in mosaiced bench seating. As she left the room, Lidia turned off the main lights, flicked a switch, which at once illuminated the mirror fragments with dancing, colourful fairy lights.

Lidia appeared after a little while bearing a tray of glasses, plates, a bottle of lemon cordial and a sponge cake.

"First, be refreshed," she said smiling broadly. "Then we shall tour the house and I shall explain to you the many features of interest."

We were mesmerized.

After our refreshments, we joined the other tour group who were now on their way down the corridor to the interior of the house. We then had a chance to look around at the reception room. Every surface was mirrored in some way and around a corner, in an alcove, was the kitchen. A fully working kitchen complete with oven, cupboards and a fridge were all covered in tiny bits of mirror, arranged in patterns and designs.

Rupert was right – it was mental.

According to our hostess she had begun mosaicing when she discovered termites were eating her house. Some of the mosaic had to be redone a few times due to the termite issue. I couldn't help feeling that this poor lady was charging people to look through her home as it was falling down around her, and using the entrance fee in a continual patch-up warfare with the termites, which appeared to be winning.

The House of Mirrors was the high-light of my Eid week, and I never did find the Kuwait wonderland depicted so tantalizingly on the promo video. I know there were Arab stallions prancing around somewhere close, but as described in a previous chapter, these beautiful things were invite only, off-limits and behind closed doors.

Some more energetic teachers sought out weekly social activities. Dolores, a vivacious South African, my short-term flat mate before Tessa moved in, had exceptional get-up-and-go. She went to salsa classes at the Hilton and joined the sailing club at Fahaheel where she learnt the ropes on a small yacht with some other expats. She invited me to join, but the idea of moving around efficiently early on a Friday morning, was an impossibility. I graciously declined.

Dolores was lively: one of those people that involves everyone around her into her drama, like the eye of a tornado. There is no real conversation just a series of announcements. It doesn't seem to matter if there is anyone else in the room, she will plonk herself down on the couch and start talking about whatever is on her mind, whether you have elicited that, or not. For a while there I was enjoying the Ivory Tower selfishly, all to myself, so when Dolores moved in, it was a bit of a shock. I could only really put up with her because I knew the situation was only temporary, as she was waiting for her single accommodation to be ready in the other teachers' building.

In small doses, I was amused by her energetic view of the world and hearing about her life, which was so very different to mine. But she had an annoying habit of ironing in the kitchen, the smallest room in the flat, during those precious minutes in the morning before school. Mornings are not a good time for me. I had my routine mapped out where I didn't need to think too much about what I was doing –

orange juice, coffee, packed lunch, gone. With Dolores there, mostly in my way in the kitchen, the weeks she was flatting with me severely tested my patience and general peace and well-being. I was happy to see her go and helped her pack.

"You should definitely move in together," said Dave, seeing sense, when Tessa and I were round at his for a cuppa. I knew that Tessa was heartily sick of living with Marjorie the chain-smoking, meat-eating telly-watcher even though she didn't voice it.

"I'm right, you know I am," Dave continued with a knowing nod and a wink, as we looked at each other.

I didn't want to plead or appear needy but when Tessa agreed to move in and I was so very grateful. The idea of another Dolores moving in, replacing the old one that had just moved out, made me miserable.

Tessa had reservations about leaving Marjorie alone, but it wasn't long before Marjorie was joined by Lisa, another South African. She was in her early twenties and had never lived away from mum and dad. She was scared to leave the house by herself, even to walk to school, so Dave, being the kindhearted friend to the weak and defenseless, saw it as his duty to be her unofficial bodyguard.

This was priceless to the casual onlooker, as she obviously annoyed the hell out of Dave with her high-pitched whining and continuous empty-headed chatter. In the same way that he had taken Tim under his good natured wing, his caring-for-the-unfortunate had again backfired, causing Dave internal frustrations, which had to be expressed. So, when I was round at Dave's place one day and saw a head-sized dent in the kitchen cupboard, I didn't ask.

Unlike some other teachers in our apartment, Tessa and I were invited to Dolores' fiftieth birthday party. Originally she had talked about hiring a boat and having a boat party for a select few, but there were horror stories of boat parties being ambushed and shut down by the police, where all on board were carted off to prison for imbibing and having a good time. The next idea was to go bowling, but that had been canned. Then there was talk of converting the very user unfriendly space on the rooftop into a Bedouin inspired lounge. The enormity of this task made it a non-starter and it stayed a great idea. We then received a message to meet at a restaurant, but that had meant no boozing at all, so instead of having friends over to her own comfortable two bedroom apartment, she decided to have a party in the basement by the pool.

A 'pool party' is what you will imagine, no doubt. But as described in a previous chapter the pool in the basement of the old teachers' building was not a pleasant place to be. It was cold down there and due to unsatisfactory ventilation smelled strongly of chlorine and socks. Florescent lighting blinked and some tinny, laptop speakers provided a background noise.

Tessa and I went, and arrived unfashionably on time. The pool area was decorated with colour photo print outs of Dolores in various poses, blu-tacked to the tiles. There were candles floating in the pool and a table with a pile of fuchsia pink iced cupcakes stacked up on a plate beneath paper cut out words *50 and fabulous!*

There were other tables laid out with enormous platters of food, labelled and wrapped in plastic. She had gone to a lot of trouble. After hanging out in the stinky gym, playing pool and chatting, Tessa and I were joined by some other teachers from school and the salsa teachers from the Hilton. A large Afro-American man in a loud oversized shirt, long shorts, baseball boots and a cap turned backwards, was there as well. He looked like a character from an Eddie Murphy film.

When the birthday girl finally made her appearance in a skintight hot pink, shiny metallic mini-dress and matching heels, she entered with a loud whoop of delight. She was made up to the nines with fake eye lashes, lashings of lip gloss and long, curved pink acrylic nails and she waved a glass in one hand. She was accompanied by other South African teachers of the same vintage who, it seemed, had all spent the afternoon at the same salon.

After greeting her guests with flamboyant air-kisses, loud *loves* and *darlings*, she shouted "Let's eat!" and tottered over to the food table, ripping off the plastic wrapping and handing out plates. From the lavish spread, it was obviously that she was expecting more than the eight people present, but she hardly let her disappointment show and continued knocking back the contents of her glass, refilling it from a bottle under the table. As she leant across in front of Mr Afro-America, he was evidently enjoying the proximity of her encased, tightly wrapped, ample rump.

"Hee, hee, you is one hell of a lady, alright, yes ma'am, mmm mmmmm, just look at that booty."

"Oh my god, you're real," said Tessa, without missing a beat. "I thought you were only in the movies, but here you are, large as life."

The point of this comment was lost on Mr Afro-America, but I had to leave the room because a suppressed laugh was forcing an explosion of Malibu and lemonade out of my nose.

For some reason Dolores wasn't the only one who decided that the stinky pool area was a great place for a party. It was the venue for K.G. teacher Mara's thirtieth - a disco theme. She had press ganged her friends into cutting out coloured card into vinyl records, musical notes, and slogans such as 'disco inferno', 'dance, dance, dance,' and 'boogie nights'. There was a lot of effort put in, but in the end, however the area was dressed up, it was still the stinky, cold pool in the basement.

Sandra and Rupert had a social network up town through one of Rupert's colleagues from home, and regularly were invited to soirees and other events. These people lived in another income bracket from us. They were teachers in top prestigious schools where the children of royalty attended. They mingled with highly paid engineers and other expats who were connected to the lucrative business of extracting oil. The wives didn't work: they lounged and lunched with other wives. Many of these people, mostly from the U.K., had been in Kuwait for ten or more years. They were addicted to the lifestyle, high on income and all talked about leaving, but you could tell they were bluffing. They had no intention of quitting.

210

Kris, a teacher at school, was an avid golfer. She made it her Friday ritual to smack small balls around on a course not far from Mangaf. One day we got chatting and she mentioned that she had seen some large lizards at the golf course where she played. Large lizards? I was immediately interested.

The following Friday, not too early, we took a taxi to Ahmadi Golf Club, Kris to play golf and me, to go on lizard safari. I channeled my inner naturalist, eager to find a sign of lizard life.

The golf club had a retro seventies feel about it in the fake wood paneling and amber glass light fittings. The cool dimness inside the club house was a welcoming respite from the intense light and heat outside.

Kris marched out to tee off at the first hole and I edged around the rough, searching for burrows. Unlike other golf courses around the world, there was no grass, just sand, grit and dust. The fairways and greens were not green but beige sand, grit and dust. The greens were manicured compacted down sand, grit and dust, which was made smooth with a little oil to hold it all in place.

There were no other golfers around. The place was eerily quiet. I felt as if I was in an actual desert looking for actual wildlife. I summoned the spirit of David Attenborough as I crept through some scrubby trees, carefully trying not to make any noise in the dead dry leaves and over-hanging branches.

I saw some minor birds, sparrows and pigeons, but no lizards. Occasionally, in the distance I would hear Kris swearing or the thwack of club hitting ball, but apart from that there was no sound – just me, breathing. I saw some holes in the ground which could have been lizard burrows, but there was no sign of life, no sound of scurry or imprints of feet, no tracks or trails. I did see an almost complete rat skeleton and some drifts of rubbish, but no lizards.

The lizards I was hoping to see, according legend, measured about a metre from nose to tip of tale. How amazing it would be to see this mini dinosaur. But after two hours or so in the blinding heat I would have been happy to see a gecko.

Sadly for me if there were lizards presumed to be living on the golf course they kept their presence a secret. I imagined them laxing out, playing a game of cards. In my head they sounded like Al Pacino.

Lizard 1: Did you see that lady? (Puts down a card in the middle of the table.)

Lizard 2: What lady? (Puts down a card.)

Lizard 1: The one walking around, snoopin'.

Lizard 3: There was the one playing golf, swears a lot. (Puts down a card.)

Lizard 1: Nah, not her. There was another one. Shifty. Not playing golf. Up to somethin'. (Puts down a card.)

Lizard 2: She probably lost somethin'. A ball maybe…. (Looks around the burrow nervously, then puts down a card.)

Lizard 1: I'm tellin' ya, she wasn't playin' golf, she was snoopin'. Nosin' around. Turnin' the heat on us.

212

Lizard 3: Relax, (takes a puff of his cigar, then puts down a card) she don't gonna find nothin' is she? I mean, we didn't leave no trail. Did we? We covered out tracks, right? And we're snug down here in this cozy joint, playin' cards. Mindin' our own business. Nothin' to worry about. Don't sweat it ……..It's your turn.

Lizard 1: Yeah, yeah, your right….. (lights a cigar from the box on the table). She won't stick around. It's gotta be fifty degrees up there. (Puts down a card.) Snap! I win.

Rupert had been running – a lot. When he arrived he was positively portly, but a combination of diet, exercise and limited booze meant that he had literally sweated off the kilos and was now a trim and fit version of himself.

He was energized by his newly acquired fitness and found out there would be a 'fun run' happening soon, which was open to all. He rallied round to get a posse together. I am not much of a runner. I don't run, but I was interested in a day out, so I put my hand up as team support. Sandra was going, also not running and the other space in the hire-car was occupied by Tim, who at twenty-one was out to win having done no training what so ever, because as he reminded everyone, he had been a semi-professional footballer. He made comments all the way about how he was going to speed past Cliff who was old and whose running days were obviously close to being over.

After relying on the sat-nav and then on Google maps we found the race start on road 30, the main drag from Kuwait City to Iraq. This road had hit the headlines in the early nineties when it was bombed by

Storming Norman, trapping and killing Iraqis who were trying to make their escape across the border. It was known as the Road of Death and here we were for the fun run.

The competitors each registered and received a number to be pinned onto their t-shirt. There was a decent sound system, so as chief team supporters, Sandra and I wasted no time and got to work dancing around, singing along to the likes of ACDC and Bon Jovi. We were interviewed by a man with a microphone and a camera for the organiser's facebook page, and although we were enthusiastic and animated our comments were not included on the final cut. We were, however, part of a high, long shot, from a drone camera, head banging away in the general crowd of spectators and participants.

Fun run flags fluttered, runners stretched, warmed up and smoked cigarettes. There was a strong wind from the west, which wafted the unmistakable stench of decomposing flesh. My first thought was that perhaps the corpses of escaping Iraqis had not been cleared up properly, but that theory was dismissed when, on a snooping mission over a nearby sand hill I discovered a dead camel and her calf, which had exploded from methane buildup in its gut. Bits of scattered dead camel littered the ground. I didn't hang around.

Rupert did quite well, finishing in the top twenty with Cliff. Tim trailed in with the final finishers looking decidedly ill and wobbly. Instead of going straight home, we decided to make use of the hire-car and checked out Sabah Al-Ahmed Natural Reserve. It was marked on the map as a green area, but when we pulled up at the gate I was surprised to see that the fenced in area was as brown and featureless as the surrounding country. I don't know why I was surprised: I was just being hopeful. We looked through the gates that were locked, then drove off not feeling that we had missed out on anything grand.

The obvious expat fun thing to do was to become a member at the Hilton health club, which by good fortune was just up the road on the coast. We wangled a 'taster day' through school early on, with no intention of becoming a member as the price tag was on the steep side, so this oasis of luxury remained an out of reach mirage.

I did, however, cheekily organise another taster day. I emailed to say that a friend and I had moved to Kuwait and were considering joining their gym. I received a delightful email in response from Anna, who was happy to 'welcome us into the Hilton family' and provide a letter of access so we could 'enjoy the full Hilton experience.'

Tessa and I settled on a date on a long stretch in between scheduled holidays and eagerly awaited our slice of heaven. The Saturday arrived wrapped in a blue sky with a refreshing sea breeze. We turned up in a taxi and pretended we were the wealthy people we were not. Entering the main hotel foyer as you would enter a cathedral or place of spiritual worship, we spoke in hushed whispers and took the lift down to the health and fitness centre.

The reception desk was dark wood panels with shelving behind containing innumerable rolled blue towels. There was no-one around apart from one man wearing an anorak done up to his chin with the hood up.

After initial greetings and awkward non-understanding, we learned that this person didn't have a clue about any introduction letter that we were expecting.

"I have surgery," he said pointing to his head, which explained why his hood was up.

"Ah OK. I thought you were just cold," I said trying to make light of the situation. "Well, we are here for a trial day. There should be a letter...... from Anna?"

"Is fifteen KD," he said. "For each person."

"Mmmm, I don't think so. We have an arrangement with Anna," I said a bit more insistently.

I saw an official looking piece of paper with the Hilton logo on it, picked it up and waved it around a bit, saying my name and Tessa's. Something seemed to click with the receptionist and he started opening draws and cupboards, shuffling through trays of paper. He found a stack of envelopes bound together with an elastic band. They were invoices addressed to other people, but he held up each one in the hope it would be what we wanted.

He called someone on the telephone. Then he held up a cell phone and a handbag and said "shuay, shuay", which roughly translates into 'wait a minute'. We deduced from his pantomime that he was not the receptionist, but he was minding the desk until the receptionist returned.

We made ourselves comfortable on some sofas and waited. The flat-screen TV showed a recent sporting event where large gold medals were handed out liberally to blobby-looking people in bright lycra and coloured running shoes. The sequence was on a loop. I watched it four or five times: the power of flickering light meant I could not look away.

After a while a smiling woman appeared. She was not Anna, and she could not find a letter, but she said we were welcome to use the beach and pool facilities, then later we could collect the letter from her at reception, which would give us access to the gym and spa. Finally, thank the lord, we were in and enjoying a whole day of luxurious self-indulgence.

Even though there are no bars or clubs in Kuwait, there are restaurants and cafes where you can share a bite with friends. There are the usual American imported eateries such as Star Bucks, McDonald's, Paul's and all the rest. Generally, I don't frequent these establishments as by doing so I would be supporting the American cultural take-over of the world. Also, I find these places overpriced, vegetarian options minimal and lacking in interest. Tessa and I tried other independent local food outlets, where the food was cheap and good but lacked character or ambiance of any kind. The Indian restaurant, a block away from the Ivory Tower, served the best masala dosa I ever had, but you wouldn't go there for a fun night out.

Local independent cafes regularly dropped off flyers to the surrounding apartment buildings to advertise their menu and opening hours. One caught my eye with a friendly description of what to expect. This café was a place to go for breakfast, lunch and dinner: it was somewhere to 'hare gout' with your friends.

It didn't take long before I realised that Kuwait was a place to make money and not spend it. There are fun things to do in Kuwait but mostly these things are expensive and mostly located a taxi ride from Mangaf. As school drained my reserves of going-out energy, life became simple and Zen-like, and I found that I hardly left the apartment at all. I didn't want to. I was quite self sufficient and I loved my down time.

Sometimes I would walk to the beach to look at the water; sometimes alone, sometimes not. During my non-work time, which was precious, I would indulge in solo past-times. I would lie on my comfy couch, feet up on the back-rest, watching the weather; watching the pigeons swoop past the window or airplanes; watching the sky change from blue to pink to orange to indigo. I intensified and extended my yoga practice. I read books. I Skyped friends and family. I danced around in my lounge, the volume on my laptop turned to max. I had sewing projects of clothes that needed taking in because I accidently dropped a dress-size through yoga, swimming and my lazy, mostly raw-food-because-I-can't-be-bothered-cooking-anything-that-doesn't-microwave diet. (*Raw Food and Microwave Cooking For One* cookbook, following soon.) I planned future travels and researched destinations on my wish list. I watched a whole heap of movies; at one point oscillating from chick flicks to documentaries on quantum physics, in the same way as your taste buds crave something sour after eating something sweet.

218

I had a lot of time, just me myself and I. I was never bored. I enjoyed my very small life: it was lush. I had redefined fun.

16

Merry Christmas!

On the countdown to Christmas I made an advent calendar for the flat.
It wasn't so much a traditional advent calendar where the countdown is
from the first to the twenty-fifth of December. Mine stopped at
twenty-three – the last day of term. I taped it up by the door and, like a
child awaiting Santa I would look at it every day, impatient to see the
passing of time. I'm not sure if it helped, but it was a colourful talking
point.

"How many days to go?"

"Oh. That many…...Are you sure? Count again. 1, 2, 3, 4…..."

The nights were cold now and the days were short and decidedly
chilly even outside my classroom, which was air-conditioned to the
max from day one. I never figured out how to adjust it and was told
that the air-conditioning for the whole school was 'centrally regulated'.
In the heat, early in the first term, a cold classroom was a bonus, but as
the outside temperature plunged, my classroom remained freezing.
Other classrooms on different floors also benefited little from the
central temperature regulator: some areas were always roasting while
others, like mine, were permanent fridges.

As December dragged, I woke to the morning alarm in the dark: it felt like the middle of the night. I bought a heater. Something I would have laughed at only a few weeks before as I sweated my way from home to school and back again. The flat had become uncomfortably chilly and I realised I was living reminiscent of my student days, wearing thermal layers, wooly hats and scarves in the lounge and even in bed, just to keep warm.

One day at the end of morning briefing, Joanne made an announcement.

"The British Embassy has allocated some tickets for their annual carol concert, so if anyone would like to go, come and see me sometime today. Thank you. That is all."

"I couldn't think of anything worse," said Tessa as she stood to leave.

"Oh where's your Christmas spirit?" said Dave, who loves Christmas and was looking forward to flying home.

Before coming to Kuwait I had pondered the idea of teaching in a school with no Christmas. Growing up in London, the run up to Christmas was so much more than just looking forward to some days off. It was a frenzy of cutting and sticking activity. I remember making Christmas cards for everyone I knew with green and red paper and glitter - lots of glitter. We painted a Father Christmas mural - red coat, black belt with a gold, shiny buckle, a bushy white beard and rosy cheeks. Father Christmas happily riding his sleigh pulled by the galloping reindeer, flying through the night sky of glittery stars and tinsel, Rudolph at the front with his enormous glowing nose. There were Christmas crackers that we had modified from the cardboard tubes of kitchen roll that the whole class had been collecting for most of the year. We made trumpeting angels, carefully cutting holes in black sugar-paper and gluing different coloured tissue paper on the back for a stained-glass window effect. An abundance of cotton-wool snowmen were placed on every surface and paper snowflakes decorated every window. There was always a cardboard post box, covered in red crepe paper with a fluffy mock-snow roof, where we could send our Christmas requests addressed simply to *Father Christmas, The North Pole*. We made cardboard Christmas trees which slotted together and stood up without the need for glue or tape. We hung the classroom with coloured streamers and paper-chains and wrote Merry Xmas everywhere. And then, of course, there was the nativity play with shepherds and kings, a Mary and Joseph and an Angel Gabriel bringing glad tidings, and the chance for even the dimmest kid to be part of something on a stage.

What would a Christmas in a Kuwaiti school be like?

Like a non-Christmas, because Christmas doesn't happen. At school, that is.

At the mall it's a different story. The malls in Kuwait are full of American owned chain-stores and I don't have to explain here the power of Disney and the global effect of a commercial Christmas where happiness is measured in cash through the till.

In the biggest mall, *The Avenues*, retail outlets all play *100 Christmas Classics* on high rotation like everywhere else dominated by consumer culture. Windows display the perfect gifts for him or her, the same display, identical in every way in every mall in every country around the world. A giant Christmas tree in a central space is decorated with coloured lights, tinsel, reflective baubles, and a number of dazzling, ribbon wrapped mock-presents are heaped tantalisingly under its branches. Santa is there too, in his mechanical form, waving hand and nodding head. "Ho ho ho" - a mirthless voice recording.

Ironically enough and in true British Christmas tradition, a pantomime was scheduled for the last week before the end of term to be performed by members of staff, but because of the general dysfunction of the school, the panto didn't actually go ahead until April. More about that later.

It was Tessa's birthday, so we decided to push the boat out and have a celebration dinner at the *Expat Café*, which had a number of favourable reviews online. We were determined to find it, although it did mean bypassing a masala dosa at our usual Indian restaurant.

In the neighbourhood, a few windows had coloured lights and *Merry Christmas* messages, but overall the place was its dingy, uninteresting self. We dodged traffic, cat carcasses and piles of rubbish on our way to the location where Google maps had directed us. Down a dark side street, back from the coast road was a glowing red, welcoming sign - *Expat Café*.

We entered through a narrow gate in the bamboo fencing and were met with the smiling faces of the owner and the waitress who seated us at an outside table close to a patio heater. The café was quirky and fun. It was a family business run by people who cared about the décor and atmosphere. Astroturf covered the ground and fairy lights were looped around the fencing and table umbrellas. There was a Christmas tree inside on the counter top and numerous other tacky bits of Christmas stuff, all shiny and glittery and necessary. Christmas classics played through the speakers.

Three ginger and white kittens dashed in and out of the shadows, hiding behind the steps, under tables and in between legs. They weren't at all concerned about the guests and were totally immersed in their game.

In the corner furthest from the door was a table of seven of varying nationalities. They spoke English together, but with accents I couldn't place. They were a lively bunch, laughing and joking as they shared their meal.

The place held that magical element that only an independent, locally owned establishment can possess: something that all the global chains aspire to, but because of their nature, will never achieve. It's hard to pin point exactly what creates the 'something right', but the *Expat Café* had it in its decorative, bitsy, charming, thrown together way.

Tessa skipped main and went straight for desert, which was admirable, and I did too. We sung 'happy birthday to you' and tucked into outrageously enormous, ice-cream laden, chocolate sprinkle covered waffles with syrup, cherries and cocktail umbrellas.

We agreed that this was our place and we would return often. It was a refreshing destination away from the malls and usual food outlets. Somewhere to come for a juice or coffee in a funky, friendly environment, with kittens. But the next time we did, it was May, and the *Expat Café* was nothing more than a red sign over the door of yet another bakala. I felt sad and guilty, that somehow our lack of patronage had been the reason for its closure.

It was now the week before Christmas and I could tell Tessa was depressed.

"Fuck," she said. "Mara has bought me a ticket for that fuckin carol concert and now I have to go," she moans.

The carols at the British embassy were a tradition – a chance for all the expat Brits to get together and share some Christmas cheer, mulled wine (non-alchoholic), a mince pie, and sing some Christmas carols, just like home. Apparently the embassy staff were wonderful hosts, but the evening of carols and cheer didn't come cheap and 'guests' were required to pay a princely sum. The 'invitation', because that was printed on the ticket, had a start time of 7.30pm with carols at 8.00pm, followed by refreshments served in the garden, and a finish time of 9.30pm sharp.

When Tessa, Mara and some other festive-type teachers arrived there was a queue stretching from the embassy front door and out of the gate as security personnel scanned all bags, coats and bodies. Once through security each guest was handed a photocopy of the words they would need to join in the singing. Then they were hurriedly ushered through to some chairs in a hall where a group of people stood at one end, smiling awkwardly at the assembling throng; obviously the choir.

The hold up with security meant that the guests were still finding a seat when the carols should have started. There were coughs and some shuffling as the lights dimmed and a nervous choir-master, aware of the delay, began the programme. The choir raced through *Once in royal David city*, then without pausing, went straight into *Christmas tree, oh Christmas tree*. He made a very short speech of welcome before *Oh come all ye faithful* at double speed. He missed the last verse of *Good King Wenceslas*, and belted, breathlessly to the finish of *Silent Night*. The lights came up and the bemused crowd, still clutching their printouts, were guided out to the garden via a side door.

"Well, wasn't that lovely," said Myrtle shoving into her mouth a third mince pie.

Adults chatted in groups and children raced around noisily, until at 9.15pm there was an announcement that everyone should make their way to the exit as the embassy was closing in fifteen minutes.

"Please make sure you take all your belongings with you when you leave, as unclaimed items will be destroyed. Merry Christmas and a happy new year."

At school Sandra decides to rev up flagging staff moral by organising a secret Santa and a shared meal for the last day of term. Bless her. The venue was the play area downstairs in K.G. She even

226

finds some speakers and a way of playing some Christmassy music. The secret Santa gifts are all piled on a table to one side, and plates of food are arranged on other tables against the wall and labelled Veggie, Gluten-free and Desert.

While she and her staff were setting up, she stopped one of the security guards trying to make off with a bag of secret Santa pressies. She said to me later that he wasn't at all remorseful, just genuinely annoyed that he had been caught. He persisted to hold a grudge into the following term and would not speak to Sandra again.

When a majority of the teachers were present, Rupert stood and said a few words, then we all gave Sandra and her team a clap and a cheer for pulling the event together. Even I left my 'bah humbug' attitude at the door and joined in with the good-hearted hubbub.

The secret Santa presents were exchanged and we helped ourselves to the shared feast with paper plates and plastic spoons. As I look around at my fellow workers I notice that there is real sense of, well, happiness. It almost felt like Christmas.

I was out of Kuwait that Thursday night on flight bound for the beaches of Goa, but Tessa didn't leave until Saturday. She emailed me a Christmas card: a photo of the dead cat from dead cat corner wearing a paper Santa hat. There was a hand drawn, cut-out speech bubble placed on the ground close to its mummified open mouth. "Merry Christmas!" it said.

17

Lying and Cheating

There was a rumour that we would be getting a visit from the Ministry of Education. The visit would mean a check on employee visas and civil I.D. paper work. I had arrived on a three month tourist visa which meant that I had to leave Kuwait every three months, and that legally I could not work.

The morning briefing went like this.

"For those of you with a tourist visa, there is no need to be anxious or upset about the ministry visit," said Cliff sincerely. "We are here to make sure that you get the support and guidance that you need, and that no-one is going to be deported…..today."

There was some shuffling and I'm sure I heard a stifled articulation of 'bullshit' before he continued.

"Some time this morning, you will be asked to leave school, go home and wait for a message from me or your head of section, for you to then return to school. I cannot say exactly when this will be, but rest assured we, the management, have your best interests at heart and there is absolutely no need to be alarmed."

I tried not to give away the jubilation at being released from my duties on the first day of the working week as I wandered up from the theatre to flag ceremony. Around school in general, despite or because of Cliff's announcement, there was a flutter of mild panic about a ministry visit which permeated through corridors and classrooms. By mid-morning the rumour had triggered management to make the call, releasing all the illegal staff who exited the premises like a flock of racing pigeons.

I escaped through the front door, shades on, hat pulled down like a fugitive in the run. Tessa was already at home when I arrived, feet up on the couch, with a cold malt-brewed beverage in hand. We were both illegal immigrants.

"It's fake beer, but I felt like celebrating! Cheers to cheating."

The ministry, unfortunately, didn't visit and the message came too soon, that our presence was required in the classroom. We didn't react immediately, choosing first to finish our drinks and snacks before slowly making our way back to school.

There were many incidents of cheating that I noticed in my time in Kuwait and on the face of it, cheating seemed to be an acceptable way of going about things. In the eighties, Kuwait had an agreement with the other oil producing nations to cap production in order to keep prices high. After shaking hands and smiling for the cameras with its OPEC mates, Kuwait then decided to open its own retail petrol outlets, *Q8* in the U.K., in order to supply as much oil and petrol as possible, while undercutting its rivals.

In sports, FIFA imposed a ban on the Kuwait football team in 2007 because of government involvement. The ban has been lifted a couple of times, but then reinstated because Kuwait just can't seem to stick to the rules.

In class, I became aware of this disregard for simple rule following when choosing sides for dodgeball. The children, as anywhere on the planet, love to get out of the classroom for a run around. The promise of golden time was sometimes a powerful tool to get things done in class. A game of dodgeball in the quad for golden time was an enjoyable reward for a well behaved class. The timing of such was crucial because the quad was more or less in use the whole day, every day. But there were small windows of opportunity for a cunning teacher to take advantage of in the teaching week.

When it comes to going to assembly or a specialist class, lining up is normally a messy, noisy business that ends up with me shouting and ordering everyone back into the classroom to start again, but when lining up is for golden time, the children become the model class. They quietly stand, facing the front, hands by their sides, not pushing or talking or mucking around. Just standing in a line.

Down in the quad I put the children in teams by giving each child a number – one or two. The ones go to their side and the twos go to their side. Simple enough. What actually happens is the children would wait to see which side their friends, or the good players, were on then happily go and join them. The result would mean that one side had most of the class, while the other side would be a handful of the, let's say, unpopular no-hopers.

More often than not the game would be postponed while they sorted themselves, or I sorted them, out which would take up most, or all, of our window of game opportunity.

Back in the classroom I would use the experience as a teaching point.

"So, who was happy with our three minutes of dodgeball?" I'd ask.

Shaking of heads and low mumblings.

"Why did we only have three minutes of dodgeball, do you think?"

"Because Ali, he cheat."

"Did he? How?"

"Because he was two and he came to one."

"Wallah Miss, I swear, I am one. You give me one. Ahmed is two."

"No, no! You say for me one, I go to one."

And so it continues. Loud Arabic voices join in all accusing each other at the same time until I say "STOP!"

Once I have regained some kind of quiet and calm I ask "Do you think that next time we go for a game, you can just be in the teams I put you in?"

"Yes Miss," they all agree nodding sincerely, down-cast eyes. And I believe them. Until the next time, when the whole scenario is played out again.

The biggest cheat in my class had to be Sara. She was quite specialized in her cheating and she didn't seem to think there was anything wrong in what she was doing. She was generally a well-behaved, intelligent, student who had a solid friend base in class. She was smiley and polite and not the sort of girl you would think was a cheat.

To encourage good work I gave out *star cards* – photocopied pictures of stars with 'good job' and a smiley face. I had a master sheet of thirty that I could copy and cut, so I always had a ready supply to hand out. I tried to give them out evenly to the whole class, so even the no-hopers would feel they had done something worthwhile. The children wrote on their names and the date it was received and kept a tally each week. The child with the most star cards at the end of the week would be *Star of the Week* and earn some golden time for themselves and two friends, and the one who had collected the most during the year, would be *Star of the Year* and win a little prize. These things work well with some kids and others, not.

I thought the star card thing was quite straight forward. I gave them out, the children wrote on them and kept them safe until the end of the week, when we had a count up. How wrong I was.

Some kids gave all their star cards to their friends and even stole them from other children to fix *Star of the Week,* to get golden time for themselves and the friends who had supplied the star cards. But Sara went one step further and started to manufacture her own.

I became suspicious at one week's count up when she presented a sizable pile of paper stars, much more than anyone else. She was Star of the Week. I allowed it because she was really a smart girl and did some good work, so I turned a blind eye – that time. But the star card production continued and by the following week I had to confront the issue. I set the class a quiet task then called Sara outside and asked her to bring her star cards with her.

She handed over a small plastic bag which was brimming with star cards. While the children were at break, I emptied the bag out on a table and perused the pile, thinking about the best way to go about addressing this obvious and blatant deception.

Some of the star cards were clearly ones that I had given her as reward for her efforts, but others were copies, where she had arranged the star cards on a piece of paper and simply photocopied away to her heart's content. She had not been particularly careful in her counterfeiting. My cards were closely cropped squares; hers were all kinds of shapes and sizes. She had even included her star card copy sheet which was glued, double thickness.

I separated the genuine star cards from the counterfeit copies and arranged them side by side on the table. The fakes out-numbered the real ones by around five to one.

"Do you want to talk to me about this?" I asked.

Sara looked at me blankly, then at the two piles.

"OK, I'll tell you what I see here," I begin. Then explain that I think she has been making star cards which of course is cheating and quite serious.

"Wallah! Miss, I swear I didn't!"

Even with the evidence in front of her in black and white she still tried to convince me that all the star cards were the genuine article. I ignored her pleadings, gave her back the handful of real star cards and put the others in the rubbish. "The point is this Sara," I said as evenly and clearly as possible. "You could be *Star of the Year* without going to all this trouble. You are able and clever enough to do it on your own without cheating."

She stopped making star cards in my class, but the following year she was up to her old cheating tricks again with her year five teacher.

I gave out *Magic Writing* books to children who wanted to write. These were simply extra, unused exercise books I had on the shelf. There were some good writers in class and I wanted to acknowledge them and get them to write more. I framed the offer in a way that, hopefully, the other not-so-capable kids would want a *Magic Writing* book too. It was not mandatory. Most of the children gabbed one, wrote their name on the front and decorated it, and told me they would write or draw something over the weekend. For most of the children this statement was a big fat lie, because I knew they had no intention of doing anything remotely school focused at the weekend. So, when Ahmed came to me on Sunday morning at registration and said that he

234

had written a story and wanted to read it to the class I was hugely impressed and agreed immediately.

I asked for quiet and announced to the class that Ahmed had used his *Magic Writing* book to write a story and that he would get five star cards for doing such great work. Ahmed began to read from the pages of his book.

"Mike Wasawski clocked in with his long time buddy and long time top scarer James P. 'Sulley' Sullivan. They were looking forward to their work of scaring little children."

I wasn't really listening at this point, but when Ahmed mentioned something about Mike's girlfriend I tuned into what he was saying and recognised that the content of the story was somehow familiar.

"Just stop there," I said gently, holding up my hand in the international gesture of 'stop'.

There was a brief murmur in the class and I continued.

"Isn't this *Monsters Inc*? A very well-known Pixar animation?"

"Yes it's *Monsters Inc*. It's my story. I wrote it," retorted Ahmed holding up his book with lines and lines of his scrawly handwriting.

There was a pause, while I thought about this. Yes indeed, he had written the story of *Monsters Inc*, but he couldn't seem to understand that it was not his story, as it had already been written by someone else, and made into a movie.

"Thank you Ahmed, we might have time for more of your story later," I said, not wanting to get into a debate I could never win. "Does anyone else have something to share from the weekend?"

I was not above reproach, I must confess. I did some lying and cheating of my own, which I wouldn't have considered doing in a 'normal' place of employment, but 'When in Rome….'

It was the run up to the Kuwait National Day holiday in February. On the calendar, two days had been allocated for the celebration and the rumour was that the ministry was going to make the call and we would be blessed with an entire free week. It had been the case the previous year and there was a buzz of anticipation.

I checked flights to Goa and spotted a couple that were still in my price range, but only if we got the full week off.

Management, in their infinite wisdom had scheduled the Saturday morning as Parents' Day, even though, as with every national holiday, everyone flies out. There would be very few parents left in Kuwait to attend.

I booked my flight for Saturday afternoon, applied for an Indian visa and counted the days.

By Thursday at close of school, no word had come from the ministry allowing for extra days off and it looked like the school would stay open after all. I picked up my passport complete with visa from the consulate office after school and started to pack. Friday I waited, and Saturday morning I was all set.

I went to school to meet with the parents, a scarf wrapped around my neck and when anyone was in ear-shot I coughed into a tissue. Some parents did come for their appointment, but, as predicted, most of the families had flown away already.

My mock illness was exemplary, and I should have received an Oscar for my performance, which was so convincing that, after only a few hours of being hunched over and coughing, I actually felt awful. I stopped by the admin office to pick up a medical certificate that I had to take with me to get a doctor's stamp of actual illness. This was the procedure for sick pay, or taking a non-scheduled day off. I left school and went to a drop-in medical centre, where I was seen by one of the doctors.

"I have a sore throat and a cough," I said, coughing. "I think I just need a few days off work to rest and recover."

The doctor listened intently, then had a look in my mouth, gently depressing the tongue with a small spatula. Then he sat down at his desk and started scribbling out a prescription, which was alarmingly extensive. He talked me through it.

"You have acute tonsillitis. I have written here," he said, pointing to the school medical certificate. "You must take three of these a day with food," he continued, pointing to the name of each medicine with his pen, "and these twice a day until they are finished."

Without being too gleeful, I thanked the kindly doctor and raced home to pick up my pack and get to the airport. There was a brief moment of panic when leaving the flat. The door of the lift opened just as I was stepping out of the front door. Luckily it was only Tessa, and she checked that the coast was clear so I could make good my escape. She took the medical certificate into school the next day and reported that I was bed-ridden, which wasn't too far from the truth, as I found it almost impossible to move from the sun lounger by the sea in my Goan heaven.

What amused me most about this episode and caused me to smile as I sipped my margarita at sunset, was the diagnosis of the medical practitioner, who gave me a stamp of 'acute tonsillitis'. My tonsils had been removed when I was a child.

I was not the only one lying and cheating on staff. Tim had developed a severe case of laringitisitis, he said. He had to go back to the U.K. for immediate surgery on his damaged esophagus, which had been brought on by his heavy consumption of fizzy drinks. His concerned colleagues in year one clucked around and organised a collection for the poor unfortunate boy. The school released him from contractual obligations and he was gone.

A couple of weeks later there were reports of sightings of the close-to-death twenty-one year old from the Midlands, in *The Avenues* mall. Kuwait is not a big place and anyone, such as a gangly, bespectacled, skinny, white teacher, who stuck out in a crowd, could hardly go unnoticed.

"He looked remarkably well, considering he had just had life-saving surgery," said one witness.

It wasn't long before the truth came out and there was an announcement at the morning briefing.

"Tim has done something quite silly," Cliff began. "As some of you may have heard, Tim has not been rushed to hospital, but has taken a position in a neighbouring school. It seems he fabricated an elaborate lie to extricate himself from his contractual duties. We have all been duped and I personally feel a bit saddened by the whole charade. The school will be pressing charges and we can only hope that he will learn from this misdemeanor."

The teachers that put up cash for his good-bye gift felt the most hurt.

"He's dead to me!" said Salma through gritted teeth. She had taken care of the young graduate and defended his lack of competence as an education practitioner with hours of support and endless resources for his classroom.

"He is quite simply useless," said Tessa who was unbelievably happy to see him go. "I would stop by his class sometimes and he would be on the carpet rolling round the floor with the children hanging off him, *The Lion King* playing on the TV at full volume. He did us all a favour. My one regret was that I actually hugged him. Ugh!"

Of course the school's threat of pressing charges would never be followed through as he, like me, was employed on a visit visa and so, as far as the ministry was concerned, did not exist.

Tim was not the only teacher to jump. Simon was first to go, having decided to accept an offer of head of science from a school in Rome. The lovely Irish music teacher didn't return from the winter break along with four others who didn't supply an excuse or reason; they just didn't show up for the new term. This was a regular thing, by all accounts. Old timers from previous years had bets on about which new teachers they thought couldn't hack it, and would just disappear. One year, as legend tells, half the staff at school went AWOL after the winter break and were never seen again. I thought about jumping. I even had a look for another job, weighing up my options, but laziness prevailed and I stayed to the bitter end.

The real extent of cheating didn't kick in properly until exam time at the end of the year. Then there were no holds barred when it came to faking it. Apparently, it is not an uncommon practice to pay for an exam paper in advance and therefore do really well in your finals when you've achieved very little all year. Students at school have been known to fork out a hefty sum for inside knowledge at the end of year exams. It's just another part of going to school: you turn up, muck about with your friends, eat lunch, go home early, pay for a tutor to try and catch you up with all the school work you've missed because you were mucking about with your friends. Then at the last minute you find a member of staff who is prepared to forgo their ethical standards for a chunk of cash and supply the exam paper, complete with answers, so you achieve the grades you need to go to university. Simple.

After the IGCSE mock exams, one science teacher in secondary noticed how similar a student's answers were to her marking scheme, right down to the note she wrote to herself, *2 marks if student draws diagram*. This mystery was never solved. Everyone shrugged. The head of secondary had no power to do anything anyway. The student was awarded an A grade - probably for copying correctly.

A year nine student was discovered with a cheat ear-piece during an exam. He was quietly reading the question to his friend in Arabic, who was then feeding him the answers through his well hidden phone. It all turned ugly for this kid when the ear-piece became wedged too far into his ear and he had to go to hospital to have it removed.

On another occasion, this time for the actual IGCSE exams, there had been a leak of exam papers, which was brought to the attention of the head of the science department. Three hours before the exam, a message had been posted on facebook, which read something like this… *Get your science answers here. Only 20KD! Make your parents proud with your awesome A. Act now! It's not too late. Get the all-you-need-for-your-science-IGCSE-exam delivered to your mail box for one easy payment.* The exam papers were changed at the last minute. There were some very disgruntled kids wandering the corridors that day.

This annoyance and indignation sometimes turned to violence, as you would expect of large, angry teenagers who were used to getting their own way. When a science teacher spoke out about an answer sheet leak, about exam papers being sold and the sham of it all, the papers were again changed at the last minute. That afternoon when she left work to drive home she found her tyres slashed and paint work scratched.

Cheating is just what happens and maybe students should be awarded marks for inventiveness and entrepreneurship, with the creative ways, using all the latest technology, they found to supply exam paper mark schemes. And it's not just the children that have ethics that are fuzzy round the edges. I encountered some parents, who were clearly not happy with the return on their educational investment, demanding that grades be changed from D to A.

"How is this possible? My son, Mohammed, he is a good boy," said a father, arms out stretched, imploring.

I start nodding, rifling through the stack of exam papers to find Mohammed's, in an attempt to justify the low mark, and show his anxious father just what I was talking about.

"Here we are. And here you can see Mohammed's exam paper," I say holding it out for him.

"This is his paper?"

"Yes."

"But he takes twenty-three per cent."

"Yes."

"I don't understand."

"Well, Mohammed hasn't really been interested in learning. He chats a lot."

The father is looking at the exam paper. He is slowly nodding, so I assume he is listening to what I am saying. Then he says "His brother he get A with everything. Mohammed he need A. His mother cry."

"OK," I say and call for back up.

Last I heard about this case was that grades were indeed changed to suit the parents' wishes. After all they are paying, I was told, so why not?

There was one mum who came in to query her son's grade because she was baffled by the C grade pass. Apparently he had been failing all year, as other marks in other subjects showed, and yet he had achieved a 62% pass mark for science in his final exam.

"I know," said his science teacher. "I was surprised myself."

"Maybe he cheat?" suggested the mother.

"Maybe," said the teacher. "Or maybe he just studied for it?"

Cheating at school was another example of the dysfunctional state in general, but Kuwait does not have a monopoly on cheats or cheating. It is just more accepted as something inevitable or even expected. Cheating happens in other countries of the world, for sure. Uganda, Algeria and Iraq, in a bid to avoid online cheating at exam time, imposed an internet black out for the whole country: an extreme measure I can't ever imagine happening in Kuwait.

18

Window Dressing

It wasn't just the kids or the inept classroom that wore me down, gnawing at my sanity. The inane demands from management were reminiscent of an Orwellian nightmare with tick-box spreadsheets of meaningless levels and grades that no-one was ever going to look at or act on. Then there were the 'looking good on paper' requirements of the BSME and COBIS applications. The school offered an image of a school that wasn't real: a cardboard cutout mock school, that in the end was all just window dressing.

At the end of term one, teachers were asked to submit names of children that were struggling, had major behavioural problems and perhaps should be at an Arabic school. We had to write an incident report on each child and submit evidence of their work and log unacceptable behaviour.

Considering that almost half the children in my class filled this *at risk* criteria I just saw a potential mountain of paperwork so just kept my head down and continued chipping away, managing as best as I could with what I had.

Nothing was said and I said nothing.

But one of my colleagues did say something. He dutifully supplied five names of at risk students who he felt were not coping, didn't have the level of English necessary to access the curriculum, so were frustrated and bored which led to disruptive, attention seeking behaviour. He diligently photographed pages from literacy, maths and science exercise books to illustrate a child's lack of ability. He included minutes of meetings with parents and strategies he had used to enable learning. Each report was typed and printed and around three pages. Just the look of it made me tired. He handed in the five reports to Cliff, the deputy head.

Can o worms.

Two months later, the teacher in question was asked to limit his list of problem kids to two. He was then told that these children were failing because of his ineptitude as a teacher. His entire teaching practice was then subjected to scrutiny from management resulting in lesson observations, planning and assessment query, and he had to spend his non-contact time observing other, more effective class teachers. He had nine years of teaching experience.

Sometime during the third term he was asked to reduce his list of two at risk children to one.

This was yet another episode of the school seen to be doing something, but actually not doing anything at all, where management sucked up to the fee-paying parents and the salary-paying school-board. The sad lack of achievement of a child was framed as the fault of bad teaching rather than the kaleidoscope of other factors in the crazy-house they called a school. But trying to deliver the British curriculum to Kuwaiti, mostly Arabic speaking children, was like asking elephants to fly: "come on now - you just flap your wings!" Most of the time teaching was like pushing shit uphill. I felt as though I was crawling on my hands and knees. How was I going to make it to the end of the year in one piece? Was it worth the cash?

The window dressing didn't stop at fictional figures on the page. The lie, the deception, the appearance of success seemed, like cheating, to be the acceptable way of doing things. Just as the hand sanitizers had been placed in school to give the look of being clean and health conscious, so the spreadsheet of grades and folders of planning on the school shared drive gave the appearance of a functioning school. Like the little man behind the curtain in *The Wizard of Oz* who pulled leavers and pressed buttons to deliver 'the show', so the school created the smoke and mirrors illusion of teaching and learning.

Sandra was part of a team at a three day schools' promotional event run by the Ministry of Education at an event centre up town. She and two Arabic staff had to set up a display table in a large hall and talk to prospective parents about the benefits of sending their children to the school.

The team were armed with glossy, colour printed flyers and mock-leather bound prospectus. The school had also provided the team with cartons of mock-leather portfolio wallets to hand out to interested parents in the hope that some free stationery would be enough to persuade. Sandra arranged the items on a purple satin tablecloth and the Arabic ladies made sure there was enough water in the urn for a day's worth of tea.

Apart from the other schools that were embarked on a similar promotional exercise, the hall was quiet and empty. The same was true of the following day. Sandra reported that she had not given away any free stationery, but chatted with her colleagues and drank a great deal of tea.

On the third and final day of the promotional event, there was a prize giving. Members of the ministry were escorted to some VIP chairs set out at the front of several rows of chairs in the hall. There was a brief welcome by an official, then the promotional teams from each school were called forward to receive engraved awards for participation, which were handed out in a satin lined, blue velvet presentation boxes. There was applause, then a chance for some questions for the members of the ministry from the participants of the event. An Arabic woman from another school stood and asked something in Arabic.

"What did she say?" asked Sandra to one of her colleagues.

"She asked 'Where are the parents?'" was the reply.

Apparently, the ministry had not publicized the event, which explained the lack of interest and subsequent empty hall, but the school received another trophy for its cabinet which was all that really mattered.

Year one seemed especially good at the razzle-dazzle of window dressing. Sasha, the year leader, had been at the school since it opened fifteen years previously. She wasn't an actual teacher, but had been friends with an actual teacher who was 'in' with the owners of the school. She had what the Kuwaiti's call 'wasta'- clout, influence, power through association. The teacher friend left and Sasha had stepped in to fill the vacant position and had been a teacher in year one ever since.

Her classroom was a wonder to behold. Five minutes in 1Yellow was like an acid trip flashback. Every inch of wall space was decorated: here is a jolly train pulling carriages across one wall; here are oversized psychedelic lollypops cut from polystyrene; here are teddy-bears having a picnic; and, oh my, is that a giant gingerbread man?

Sasha was not a native English speaker and continually amused Tessa with her choice of spelling. 'There is a *meating* in the library', one message read. And 'The queen lives in *Englande*.' And 'Elephant is *beg*'. And 'This person is *famouse*'. But amusement turned to annoyance when Tessa discovered that Sasha had blatantly copied all her mid-year report comments and used them for her own class, irrespective of how appropriate they were.

"She's used the one I wrote for Mohammed in my class, who is a little shit, for Mohammed in her class who is actually a good kid," Tessa said incredulously. "How does she think that's OK?"

Most of Sasha's class were good kids. Her class was handpicked. Only the brightest, best and most well-behaved made up the class of 1Yellow. The rest of the children who were not bright or well-behaved were distributed among the other classes in year one of the newly arrived teachers. And so it was that Tessa acquired 1Orange.

"I couldn't understand why my class were such a rabble of snotty, grubby Bedouin kids who couldn't sit straight or hold a pencil, and Sasha's class were this bunch of angels. Every time I past her door, there they were sitting there quietly copying from the board – the dream class!" sighed Tessa.

But this seemingly model class was again just a pretence. When Tessa was asked to cover 1Yellow for a morning while Sasha was out, she discovered the truth.

"The kids don't know anything," she confided. "They sit there, quietly copying, but there's no actual learning going on."

At a planning meeting, the primary school were told that there would be a Super Hero week. This was not, as I wrongly thought, a week for the children to discover the origins of their favourite comic book character, but rather a celebration of real people who have contributed something worthy to humanity. Each year group had to come up with a person of note and a plan for a week's worth of activities.

I met together with the other year four teachers and we decided upon the Dalai Lama who continually advocates for peace. What greater super hero could there be than that? But a couple of days before Super Hero week, we were informed that the Dalai Lama was not an acceptable super hero because he is a spiritual leader and therefore not within the set ministry guidelines.

Year three planned to celebrate the work of Thomas Edison; year six, Marie Curie; year five, Albert Einstein and year two, Henry Ford. Year one settled on the Wright brothers.

In the year one planning meeting Sasha was in her sparkly, Disneyfied element.

"Then the children can make models of airplanes," she gushed, "and we can dress up as air hostesses, and, you, Mr Tim, can be the pilot!"

Tessa tried to understand how dressing up as a flight attendant could possibly relate to the pioneers of aeronautics.

"And we can invite the parents to a shared lunch, and order in McDonalds, because the Wright brothers were American and McDonalds is American food!" Sasha continued without pausing to breathe.

Sure enough, on the first day of Super Hero week in year one classrooms, various models of airplanes had started to appear. Tessa saw the opportunity in her class for a 'show and tell'.

Tessa: Mohammed, tell us about your airplane. How did you make it? What is it made from?

Mohammed (shrugs): Ummmmm.

Tessa: Who helped you? Your mum? Your dad?

Mohammed: Ummm.

Tessa: OK. Is there anything you would like to say about your airplane? It is a very good model.

Mohammed: I go to bed. I wake up. Is there. I don't know.

Tessa: Thank you Mohammed. Does anyone else want to share?

While Tessa was waiting for a response from someone in her class, there was a knock at the door and Sasha popped her head in.

Knock knock. "The tailor's here," she said brightly.

Tessa was confused, wondering what it had to do with her when Sasha, still with her head around the door said "You must come now".

Tessa looked at the thirty children in her class, and assured Sasha that she most definitely could not 'come now' because she was teaching.

"OK," Sasha replied, and her head disappeared from the door. Moments later a large, heavily made up woman, dressed entirely in purple burst into the class.

"The tailor," said Sasha's head which had reappeared around the door before disappearing again.

The tailor smiled at everyone and greeted the children in Arabic. She then indicated that she needed Tessa to stand, which she did. Still not fully comprehending the situation, Tessa held out her arms to the side as she was asked to do. The tailor reached under each arm, wrapping her tape-measure round her bust and recording the measurement on a notepad. She took several other measurements of

Tessa's body, much to the amusement of the children, then said 'Shukran' and left.

The culmination of Super Hero week was Thursday afternoon. It was a sweltering day and the year one classes sat outside in their class rows, with their model airplanes of various shapes and sizes, in the blazing sun on the neighbouring Astroturf field. Parents arrived and the teachers all wore their made-to-measure flight attendant outfits.

Rupert, who was in a pilot's uniform, welcomed everyone to the event and made references to 'high-flying achievements' of the staff and children and how they had all emulated the Wright brothers' unflagging efforts to get the show 'off the ground'. Most of the parents, whose English was marginal at best, did not understand the subtleties of Rupert's light-hearted parallels, and talked among themselves throughout the address.

The food was delivered from McDonalds and the children did their best to eat the chips, burgers and ice-cream without making too much mess, before leaving with their parents. The maids were on hand with black bin-liners and brooms.

The belated staff Christmas panto was another puzzling, but colourful extravaganza of little substance: a Sasha/ Salma collaboration in which some well-known story characters and themes were chewed over, swallowed then thrown up in a vomit of nonsense.

I don't even know where to begin with the breakdown of this particular debacle – there was so much wrong on so many levels. It would be a great starting point for a sociology thesis on the fundamental fuckedupness of the world.

Anyway, the following will give you an idea of what I mean.

Enter the Mad Hatter (Salma) who dances down from the back of the theatre and in a singsong voice explains the magic properties of her hat – it tells her stories.

She then introduces Charlie, from the Roald Dahl classic, who is presented as having dinner with his family. Then he goes to sleep and dreams of winning a golden ticket which will give him ownership of Willy Wonka's chocolate factory and save him from the misery of poverty.

Stick with this. It gets better.

The Mad Hatter tells the audience he is going to go on a journey and will meet a beautiful girl with long blonde hair.

Charlie theatrically wakes, yawns and stretches and tells the audience that he has decided to go on a journey to find the golden ticket. He meets Goldilocks who is out wandering in a forest and suggests they walk together, get jobs, get married, have children and find the golden ticket.

They come across a 'help wanted' sign and get interviewed by a lady who apparently owns a sweet shop. She asks Goldi and then Charlie if they would eat her sweets if they were given the job. The audience is involved in this dilemma.

Charlie and Goldilocks: Should we eat the sweets?

Audience: Yes!/ No!

Neither Charlie nor Goldilocks get the job in the sweet shop, because they are untrustworthy, so they continue on their journey. They subsequently come across the expected home of The Three Bears and go through the porridge, the chair, then the up the stairs to bed.

I don't have to underline here the cringing innuendo of "This one's too hard. This one's too soft. This one's just right."

The bears, of course, come home and discover the home-intruders are still in the house. This dramatic moment is treated with glove puppet surprise from all performers and Goldilocks is accepted into the bear family.

Charlie continues his quest.

Enter Ma Baker who is cooking the gingerbread man. The gingerbread man, of course, gives Ma and Pa Baker the slip and he runs around the auditorium chased by a number of staff who are disguised in masks and costumes reminiscent of a sexually deviant subculture.

The Mad Hatter announces that everything that has been presented so far is just a dream and that dreams come true and you must hold on to your dreams to make them come true.

So, Charlie theatrically wakes up and yawns again and crosses the stage where his family is still pretending to eat soup.

This is when Grandpa Joe gives Charlie the Wonka bar and Charlie finds the golden ticket. Then the Oompa-Loompas appear holding the giant Styrofoam lollypops usually found in Sasha's classroom, and they sing along to the Oompa-Loompa song from the Willy Wonka movie.

Still with me? OK.

Willy Wonka enters bearing an astonishing likeness to Ozzy Osbourne and accepts Charlie's golden ticket in exchange for his famous chocolate factory.

This is the end. Everyone is now dancing round on the stage to Pharrell William's party hit ,*Happy* – The Three Bears, Goldilocks, the strange lady sweet shop owner, the Oompa-Loompas, the dogging fraternity, the gindgerbread man, Ma and Pa Baker and the Mad Hatter.

Please god let it be over, I remember thinking.

The whole school is subjected to this torture from K.G. to secondary and I'm sure that each individual child, in their own way, was as baffled as me.

The staff panto wasn't the only theatrical use of the theatre. In the stairwell down to the theatre hung photographs of school productions past. Each was labelled with title of the show and the year it was performed. When I was there, the proposed production was the all singing, all dancing *Mary Poppins* for years four to eleven.

The cast was auditioned and rehearsals began. The director, drama teacher for secondary, was a princess. He was one of these men I was sure was gay even though he was married with two kids. His style of performance was to try for a Hollywood musical extravaganza reminiscent of the 1940s, where there are a handful of central characters with speaking parts and mic'd up singing solos to hold the thing together, and a whole heap of various costumed chorus lines, made up of the not so talented kids who just want to be on stage.

Frances, who had been at school the previous year wisely told me not to encourage my class to take part because the class teachers were required to chaperone the children on performance night. The last thing you really wanted to be doing during after school hours was corralling hyped up kids in a corridor for two hours until their thirty seconds of theatrical triumph.

With that in mind I tried to dissuade the boys and girls in my class from participating, but the lure of stardom was too strong for some. On the up side, they had to skip class to go to rehearsals so I didn't lose out completely.

The drummer had quit. The band for the show now consisted of a bass guitarist who was a year nine student and a keyboard player, Gwendolyn who was the music teacher for lower primary and KG. She was old and thin with a nest of bright orange hennaed hair piled up on top of her head. She had a high-pitched wavering voice and over enunciated her words like an Edwardian lady in the era of afternoon tea, when gals had spirit if they refused to marry.

Gwendolyn was the music teacher for Tessa's class. As specialist teacher, she was supposed to take control of the children for her music lessons, freeing up the class teacher for prep or planning. But after Gwendolyn tiptoed into 1Orange for the first time - singing 'Doe-a-deer' and grinning round at the children, nodding that they should join

256

in, then sitting down next to the whiteboard where she drew a treble clef and asked the children what is was - Tessa knew that she could never leave her alone with her class. She would die.

Sandra, seizing an opportunity for rock legend status, volunteered for the challenge of show drummer and enthusiastically learnt the drum beats for each song. She practised tirelessly day and night with her drumsticks on every surface. She had the slow one two three waltz of 'Favourite Things', and the marching band beat of 'Spoonful of Sugar' down in no time. The other songs were coming along nicely and were recognisable to some degree. She loved it.

Down in theatre, one day at band rehearsal.

"Let's try 'Supercalifragilistic' one more time, and Sandra, could you play with a little less *gusto* this time," said Gwendolyn, seated at the piano. Her half-moon spectacles perched on her nose, the decorative chain looped round her neck in case they slid off. She peered at the sheet music on the stand in front of her and nodded her head as she counted, "One, two, three, four," then sang in her warbly little voice "Supercalifragilisticexpialidocious, even though the sound of it is something quite atrocious, if you say it.....No, no, no. STOP!" She put her hands to her hears the way soldiers do when they are near an exploding canon. "I can't bear it!" she continued. "The noise!" she wailed. "It's damaging my ears! I can't go on. I'm sorry; you are going to have to find someone else." And with that last utterance, she fled the auditorium and was not seen for the rest of the week.

Luckily for the production and Sandra's drumming debut, another music teacher stepped into the position vacated by Gwendolyn and the show went on. Parents were entertained, although they chatted and filmed the whole thing on their phones. They waved at their children: some waved back and others did a sterling job of ignoring them.

The school production phenomenon was a razzamatazz distraction to what was really going on. Its purpose was to showcase achievement; to demonstrate to the fee-paying parents how well their little geniuses were doing; to dress them up in shiny costumes; put English words in their mouths and make them dance on a stage like trained animals in a circus. This style of show had little to do with the children or their learning. But the following year something a bit different happened; a change from the *Mary Poppins* style musical.

"We could do a talent show?" suggested one of the secondary teachers.

Fiery daggers shot from the drama teacher's eyes.

"We can't do a talent show with these kids," he said. "It would be awful. The staff would have to perform as well to make it half-way decent for the parents. If there's going to be a talent show instead of a piece of real musical theatre, I am having nothing to do with it."

There was an awkward pause before Jenny, one of the science teachers, a young, idealistic Irish woman saw an opportunity to make things right.

"I'll do it," she said, without thinking. "I'll run auditions and see who's keen."

"Fine," said the drama teacher in the tone and manner of someone who was making a point as he flounced out of the meeting.

Auditions were held and eight acts tried out in the theatre. There was a girl who sang and played piano, but could only really sing. There were two boys who did a mash-up of Adele songs, but had learned them each in a different key, which was fine until they started to sing together. There was a dance group of five – two at the front and three at the back, where the two at the front kept turning round to see what the three at the back were doing. There was a rapper who couldn't sing so he got his friends to do the singing bit in between his raps. There were a couple more singers, a guitar player and some break-dancers.

"At least they showed up," said Jenny when I asked how it was going. "They're going to need a hell of a lot of rehearsal to get anywhere near performance level."

My mind phased back to the talent shows put on by a drama teacher friend in New Zealand. The school talent shows were legendary in the small country school where even the heats leading up to the final were electrically charged with outstanding gifted singers, dancers and musicians. The school hall would be packed with hopeful family, friends and members of the community, who were there to support, cheer and have a rollicking good night out. Some of the talent show finalists went on to forge a life out of their performing. It was a chance for the kids who were not academically inclined to show what

259

they were good at. The talent show was all about the kids – for the kids, by the kids, a celebration of their talent and skill.

Not so here in Kuwait. The student who won the talent show, the singer/guitarist, was mediocre at best, even with hours of rehearsal and extra music lessons. But she was hailed as the next Selena Gomez and awarded a prize during flag ceremony in front of the whole school. It was like the nurses at the medical centre thinking they were doctors. The Kuwaiti mirror of reality reflected a skewed image back. Once again the bar was lowered to accommodate the actual standard and the shiny, glittery, insubstantial facade was all that really mattered.

Perhaps the ultimate piece of window dressing was the graduation ceremony for year eleven leavers. The venue was the event centre at the swanky Radisson Blu hotel, up town. Students hired caps and gowns, usually reserved for actual graduation from a university degree or diploma, and behaved as if they had actually achieved something great. At school they took photos of each other all dressed up and posed like scenes from *High School Musical*. All secondary staff were expected to attend on a Friday night and the dress code was formal. There were speeches, large floral arrangements and a buffet style banquet. Proud parents witnessed their children receiving cardboard tubes tied with coloured ribbon, with handshakes, words of congratulations and smiles. These kids hadn't even sat their exams yet.

19

Rubbish

There are a surprising number of trees here in Kuwait. I tend not to notice because they are covered in a layer of dust and absorbed into the general beigeness of the cityscape, but there they are, beside the roads, in vacant lots, public spaces and private gardens.

Tough thorny trees, date palms and hardy shrubs speak of an underground water system in a river delta that is fertile and potentially productive. As proof, the vacant land behind the school was, until quite recently a section of allotments, which can be clearly seen, green and abundant, on Google Earth. And on my walk to school each morning my flagging spirit was uplifted by a small rocky garden beside an apartment block, which was leafy and carefully tended.

There is a theory that the historical origin of the Garden of Eden is located only a few kilometres somewhere off shore in the Gulf, at a confluence of four rivers the Tigris, Euphrates, Pishon and Gihon: a mythical paradise now at the bottom of the sea, out of view and reach.

The irony of this idea appeals, with or without solid scientific data, that Kuwait in a parallel universe could be a garden - a utopia of lush sustainability. With access to water and fertile dirt and a relatively small population, Kuwait has the potential to be a model state where riches from oil production could be distributed to fund forward thinking projects to enhance the lives of the people. As one of the richest countries on the planet you would think there might be some sort of government funded environmental programme for green living; with a view to lessen the impact of global fossil fuel consumption; some innovation of how to clean up the mess made by oil and plastics that have been released into oceans and seas; to show some responsibility to the world; to finance some payback for the wealth generated from oil found in your own back yard.

On a domestic level, there doesn't seem to be any central governmental plan for the environment, public spaces, housing, or anything: apart from safety warnings on the motorways such as 'drugs = death' or 'watch the road', that I assume are not just some random graffiti from a caring citizen, but a message for the community from the powers that be. The building projects seem to be mostly focused on retail shopping and eating - malls and restaurants – where the inside space is glossy and gleaming and no-one notices that outside is an uncared-for mess.

Kuwait is a place of car culture. People generally drive everywhere because of the climate and because they can. Petrol is cheaper than bottled water and only the underclass immigrant workers walk or take the bus. In the rest of the world resources are stretched to the limit, but here in this teenie tiny country there is a phenomenal surplus of wealth.

But it is relatively new wealth, and a country is like a person in the way it reacts to change. Before the discovery and the incredibly swift global dependency on oil, Kuwait was a blip on the map: a chunk of the Arabian Peninsula, which was parceled out after the end of the second world war as a strategic British outpost and protectorate. The people scratched out a living from the land and the sea. But then oil was discovered and everything changed. People who had been living on next to nothing suddenly had a share in a huge cash bonanza.

Parallels can be drawn between the people of Kuwait and Viv Nicolson, a working class woman from Yorkshire, England, who became a household name overnight in 1961, after winning 152,000 GDP on the pools. Her experience was immortalised in a book entitled *Spend, spend, spend!* (which was made into a play for television and West End theatre). Viv was so thrilled at her good fortune, the equivalent to 3.5 million pounds today, that she quite simply blew it all on luxury items. She spent the lot in three years.

And so, like Viv, this insignificant country got rich quick.

In the ghetto where I lived, it was easy to forget that this is not a third world country. Or rather, that this is a third world country, but with oodles of cash. Like Viv, the people who inherited the oil rights that lifted them and their families out of poverty so dramatically, are understandably interested in acquiring all the trappings of wealth – the high end clothing labels, jewellery, cars, houses, shoes, handbags and travel. In fact, all those glossy advertisements in airline magazines are aimed at Kuwaitis and people like them, blatantly using the imagery of affluence to sell them their desirable lifestyle.

Present day Kuwait displays all the symptoms of capitalism, commercialism, greed and the inevitable hegemony direct from America. There is no forward thinking. No vision of global sustainability. No clean green utopia. No exciting new way of doing things. Just dust, big houses and cheap apartments, malls, roads, cars and an imported social underclass to serve the elite.

Most immigrants in the social underclass are from India, Sri Lanka and the Philippines, here for the potential of increased income and to improve the lot for their families. Teachers at school have a slot with the other immigrants in the social structure of things. Kuwaitis are at the top of the heap, then other Arabic people are in the stratum below. The white expats fit in below the Arabs, followed by brown skinned immigrants at the bottom.

Up town at a university, Tessa's rugby team was playing in the final tournament of the year. I had gone along to show support and cheer in the crowd. During the afternoon I had a chance to wonder around the impressive campus and spotted a banner in the reception area which read 'Servants are people too'. This said it all.

It took a while to acknowledge the social structure and to accept that 'it's just the way things are'. I had to suck it up and to keep remembering that I was here to do a job and that is all.

From my window at the old teachers' building I watched a slice of life in this little corner of Kuwait. As with my previous dwelling at the

Ivory Tower, the view was uninhibited by another building and allowed for some empty headed voyeurism across a square of beige dirt.

There was a derelict, mud-brick house – maybe two. It was hard to tell as the walls had crumbled to a pile in the middle causing a mini, hilly landscape, which was also a dumping ground for household rubbish and car tyres. To the right and left of the derelict house, car-owners had decided that this was their car park. Another derelict mud-brick house was further over to the left, but this one showed signs it was clearly still inhabited because of the washing on the line and collection of satellite dishes on the roof.

Looking to the right of my window was an actual road, which had been partially tar-sealed recently. The road ran along the rear entrance of an Arabic school marking the second side to the square, before curving left to make the third side bordered by apartment buildings in a mirrored repeat of my side directly opposite – parked trucks, buses and cars and piles of rubbish and tyres. The fourth side of the square was a four-lane highway.

In the desert of space between apartment buildings and roadways was another derelict mud-brick house and what looked like a concrete bunker. Scattered here and there in the emptiness were fuchsia-pink mini skips - some with a *leafy tree on verdant pasture* picture, some without - where cats and people scavenged. A cluster of dusty trees clung to the edge of the space by the highway and random power lines sagged around the dwellings and looked useless. Opportunistic motorists often took a diagonal short-cut across the wasteland to get from the corner at our building one side, to the four-lane highway at the other.

This empty space was, of course, used for cricket, football matches and other activities. Men trundled gas bottles on handcarts and children zoomed up and down on bicycles. The road by our building at the back of the Arabic school was also popular with drag-racers who left plentiful tyre-marks and filled the air with noxious rubber, screeching and dust.

I observed families on afternoon picnics. They would drive to the middle of this dirty wasteland and arrange themselves on blankets. What were they thinking?

Mum: Well, this is lovely.

Dad: Are you sure you wouldn't like to be closer to the pile of tyres?

Mum: No, here is just perfect. However did you find such a place?

Dad: Ah, ha ha, I suppose just have a gift for knowing.

(Drag racers pull off successive slides and doughnuts.)

Mum: Ahmed, take care of your sister and don't go too close to the road. (Cough, cough.)

Dad: It's great to get out for a family picnic isn't it, love?

Mum: Yes, darling. We should do this more often. Here, give me a hand with the blanket and I'll put a falafel on your plate.

Dad: Oki doki. Ahhh. This is the life. It's just like the beach but without the water! Haha.

Yes, just as in *Club Tropicana* 'all that's missing is the sea' and indeed the picnic spot was exactly like the beach. The beach in Kuwait, that is.

The sand was not the silky golden or white sand of tropical far off havens. It was grit. It was grit with chunks of rock/ cement/ broken glass/ plastic pieces. Different coloured plastic bags rolled around in the sea breeze, with the remains of take-away meals still in the happy wrapping.

The gritty sand also served as a toilet for the out-of-control feral cat population. On my frequent weekend walks to Al Kout I would have to look away when I noticed toddlers digging with their fists, then finding something they think could be tasty, and popping it in their mouths. I would look around for a parent or care-giver. Was I the only one around to put the pieces together? It seemed so.

At the beach there was a hand drawn sign urging passers-by to recycle. It had the appearance of age. The blue permanent marker had faded and rust marks from the metal sheet were bleeding through the flakey white paint. A tiny planet Earth could just be made out surrounded by some triangular arrows, the international visual cue to 'do the right thing'. Rubbish that had been blowing around the beach and the footpath had come to rest on the supporting posts at the base of the sign.

If this was a government initiative it was sadly lacking. My feeling was that it had been a school project years ago, that was done as a half-hearted P.R. exercise, then once the press photos had been taken, the project had been abandoned leaving this aging sign as a silent witness. Or, perhaps, years ago Green Peace pointed an accusing finger and told Kuwait to shape up on the environmental front, so someone, with a conscience and a pen that worked, drew this recycling sign. But the real tragic comedy of the inadequate recycle signage was its close proximity to the refinery and the untold environmental damage being done there day after day. Sometimes you could taste the petrol in the air.

In spite of the plentiful wheely-bins up and down the promenade at the beach, people that picnicked still left their litter where they had been sitting. Piles of carelessly discarded packaging was blown into drifts, got caught in bushes and inevitably ended up in the sea. The clean up was done by a team of Kuwait's road sweepers.

Sweeping up rubbish was the job of immigrant men in yellow overalls. They could be seen at Al Kout beach and along the road sides with a brush and shovel, scooping up rubbish and carefully emptying it into a wheely-bin in a futile effort to clean up. There are a surprising number of road sweepers in Kuwait, a job that has to be the most pointless and thankless in the world, as there always seemed to be rubbish everywhere. With no public education or general thought of reducing rubbish at consumer level, the road sweepers of Kuwait will always be on the losing.

On the other hand, they would always be in a job. If you were looking for a job outside, where nothing much was expected in terms of results, well this could be the job for you. You just walk around all day occasionally sweep something up and put it in your bin, then wander round a bit more. This could be the ideal job for a slacker like me, I thought, as I watched the slow, half-hearted movements of one of these road sweepers pass by. I could certainly do that job for a bit; no worries, no responsibilities, no kids, no planning, no reports, no parents, no ridiculous expectations of children's capabilities.

On the upside, road sweepers got first dibs on the recyclables. Everyday a small flatbed truck pulled up outside our apartment and a couple of men loaded on bundles of cardboard and bags of cans, weighing them first on a set of scales. Clearly this was a money making exercise and not purely the result of environmental sensibilities. The smallness of the operation suggests it was a grassroots business and not a service of the town council or government agency. It also suggests that there must be enough money paid for the collection of the bundles and bags to make it worthwhile for the men to invest their time and effort. Or maybe they were just caring environmentalists doing their bit.

The cracks were starting to show. I made the mistake of looking in the mirror one day in the women's toilets at school. Fluorescent lighting is never your friend, but I must say that I looked every bit as old as my fifty years and then some - which was a shock. Under my eyes the dark bags sagged, taking over the entire eye socket, dragging the skin down to my sunken cheeks. The lines, once happy laugh-lines as I remember, around the mouth, above my eyebrows and at the corners of my eyes, were now hard drawn into a frown. My hair seemed greyer and stuck up at weird angles where it had escaped my elastic hair tie, looking more like feathers than hair. Was I morphing into Cliff? Like Cliff, I certainly was displaying all the characteristics of a stork chick. Permanent tiredness, despite early nights, was fixed on my face.

I seemed to be absorbing the ugliness of Kuwait; the colourlessness, the carelessness, the madness, the noise, the traffic, the call to prayer, the swirling litter, the shouting billboards, the grit in my sandals, the dust in my lungs. I was becoming part of it all.

I sighed.

The person in the mirror looked like she had had enough. She had lost her sense of humour: the one thing she could rely on to endure anything, had gone. The endless repetition of barking instructions, of ceaseless calling for quiet, of breaking up fights, of painfully slow step by step explanation and demonstration, of watching lessons fall apart, of high-pitched squeals in the too-small space of a classroom, resonating from wall to ceramic wall through the skull and resounding around the brain.

I realised I was taking the classroom home with me each day and holding it, and the madness in my head. The dramas of the day would play out again and again like an MTV high-rotation video behind my eyes. Sleep was twitchy.

The morning alarm would shock me into consciousness. My brain still active from the night before was mechanically nutting-out the problems of telling the time or prepositions or using the past tense or figuring out a new seating plan to separate the trouble makers or how I was going to explain to a parent nicely that their child needed urgent psychiatric help. There seemed to be a million things in my head all at once. It was exhausting.

Surrounded by dust and ugliness I craved natural forms. I missed the smell of dirt and freshly cut grass and flowers and bees and butterflies and the smells of things living and growing. There are private gardens behind walls in the more affluent neighbourhoods, but not so much in Mangaf where people generally live in apartment buildings rather than private homes.

There was, however, one small garden that someone had made purely for decoration and it was situated in a carpark/ vacant space of disused beige dust. I passed it on my way to work every day. The purpose seemed to be to designate an area in which a small motorboat was parked on its trailer. Obviously, the owner of the boat loved it so much that he or she had made a garden for it to sit in when it wasn't in the water. The garden had real grass – squares of turf had been laid down on the beige sand. Red house bricks edged the lawn in a perfect rectangle around the boat, and sunflowers grew straight and tall in pots at intervals inside the perimeter. The effect was heart-warming and a little bit mad; a demonstration of love and care that made me smile.

Although gardens are rare, there is a culture of giving flowers in Kuwait and florists are as abundant in retail centres as the chocolate, cake and gift shops. The florists window displays are elaborate, colourful and ultimately fake. Instead of celebrating the natural colours and shapes of various blooms, flowers are dyed and stems are twisted into angular arrangements that conjured cries of pain.

Occasionally at school, I was the recipient of a plastic wrapped dyed rose or carnation given by one of the children in my class. One time, a sad, droopy rose that had seen better days, lay on my desk. I had forgotten to put it in water, but it was probably past that point when it arrived in class. After I had extended thanks and gratitude for my gift, I just ignored it. Then, before break, one of the boys approached the dead rose and, without saying a word, mimed a theatrical resuscitation with an imaginary defibrillator to try and bring it back to life.

I missed my cat. I had to re-home her when I left New Zealand and I missed her furry company. There were thousands of feral cats that lived in and around the pink skips, but these animals were not cute kitties you would want to get up close to and cuddle. However, a teacher at school, who lived in the apartment directly opposite ours in the old teachers' building, decided to take in a pregnant female which was friendly enough but meowed long and loud in the corridor.

The cat had her kittens in the apartment and was allowed to come and go freely to the skip and derelict house and back to curl up on the couch with her offspring.

"She's so smoochy," said the cat lady one morning while we waited for the lift, "especially when she comes in at night. But sometimes she gets so greasy, I have to give her the once over with a baby-wipe."

In class the children were learning to draw a bar chart to present collected data. We talked about pets and found out who had what.

There were the usual cats and dogs, fish, rabbits and hamsters. There were also snakes, axolotls, lizards, a lama, sheep, camels and parrots. There were reports of other, more exotic animals such as lions, cheetahs and tigers. I have no idea if these reports were based on truth. One boy said that he wanted a monkey because he was bored with the animals he had.

The relationship with animals as pets suggested that they were viewed as another status symbol. A mum of one of Tessa's children wanted a pet cat. Tessa, who spent her holidays volunteering at animal rescue centres and would quit teaching to be a vet, suggested she adopt one of the many kittens that were so plentiful out on the street and give it a loving home. All these feral cats needed was good food, inoculations and a dose of de-wormer to turn skinny wretched vermin into household, inside-only, affectionate purry pets. She had ignored Tessa's words as if she were a bit dim and talking nonsense.

"I want an English cat," she said. "You can arrange for me? I will bring it here."

March, April, May.

I looked at the empty eyes in the grubby mirror looking back at me in the women's toilets at school.

March April May. I just had to get through the next few months.

March April May.

March April May became my mantra.

20

The last laugh

It's easy to have a laugh at Kuwait's expense. I did, often. There was so much to laugh at - the inadequacies, half-arsed attempts, the facile surface value of things, the glossed over cracks in structure, the yet-to-be-properly-formed or thought through, the over-packaging, the tragic comedy, the struggle of opposing elements that will never be reconciled, the extremes.

"I don't know if I can survive in the real world," I confessed to Tessa. "You're my measure of sanity and I think you've lost it. What hope is there?"

The school year was hurtling toward its final day. The children had finished their exams and had gone. The classrooms were echoey with the sound of maids, lounging in the stairwell, huddled round cell phones, talking loud Hindi, Sinhalese and Tamil, and laughing. The empty space still held shadows of the children; tape holding a corner of torn coloured paper from a wall display; a broken piece of a rubber aimed at someone's head now hugged the edge of the room; grubby grey classroom furniture heaped up in the middle; a still un-emptied rubbish-bin full of hand outs, lesson plans, disposable cups and broken rulers; the heights of the girls and boys sketched on a wall.

A tattered piece of green balloon reminded me of the final day with my class. I had wanted to end on a positive note, so had planned the day around some golden time, some shared food and a celebratory presentation of Star of the Year. I had bought some little battery operated candles as prizes for the deserving, and put them in pretty gift bags. While the children were at break I blew up some coloured balloons for a bit of an ooh-ahh surprise when they returned to class. The balloons rolled around the floor in their jolly colourful roundness.

My balloon surprise deflated when, in the three minutes I stepped out of the classroom, two of the naughty boys popped all the balloons with sharply pointed pencils. So when the rest of the class came back, all that was left was bits of plastic scattering the floor. So much for the ooh-ahh moment.

Where once fights, shouts and laughing had filled the tiled corridors, there was now a disquieting quiet where the hum of air-con and the plink-plink of ill-fitting fluorescent lighting tubes flicking on and off were audible like never before. Distant music from various teachers' classrooms drifted as if from a ghost world. The teachers were no-where. They came to sign in and then they left. Teachers mostly kept out of the way, doing what was required and hiding in case they were asked to do extra. Or was that just me?

There was stuff we needed to finish – busy-work for teachers. We had to enter exam results onto the reports and add the data to a spreadsheet in a folder marked with our class name. It was all prettily colour coded, but I wondered who it was for. At the start of the year I had not been privy to such a document. I had the feeling again, that it was all just for show.

It was Ramadan, which meant we were treated to a wonderful reduction in work hours; a very cruisey 8.30 a.m. start to a 1.00 p.m. finish as decreed by the Ministry of Education. Ramadan is a national religious celebration that lasts a month, where Muslims fast during daylight hours then get together with family and friends for feasting and good times between sunset and sunrise.

I was shopping for my regular supplies at the Sultan supermarket across the road from school on the first day of Ramadan. I should have postponed when I saw the number of cars in the car park and the lack of available shopping trolleys, but I had already stepped through the threshold of the store and was committed to my purpose. The place was packed. I had experienced a similar crazed, shopping panic in London in the run up to Christmas, where there seems to be an instinctive rush to grab what you can now because somehow everything was closing and there was no way you could ever get food ever again for the rest of your life. The crowd of panicked shoppers scooped arm-loads of products from shelves into baskets and trolleys and swooped down on anything that was advertised as a 'special offer'. Stressed out employees were working at double speed to restock shelves as the trolleys trundled past emptying them as quickly as they were filled. Children were ordered to run ahead and retrieve items located further down an aisle while there was still time.

The queue at the checkout was a mile long. Even the express queue required some deep breathing and an exercise in patience. When it was finally my turn I smiled at the check-out assistant and made a comment about the shop being so busy.

"It's Ramadan," she said without looking up as she scanned my items, "there's a lot of hours in the night."

Apparently, most of those night-time Ramadan hours were spent eating, making up for the lost eating hours of the day, which seemed to be missing the point of fasting.

We still had to pack up our classrooms, chuck out anything we didn't deem useful for the following year and store useful stuff in body-sized metal trunks. With three weeks to roll in this new child-free routine it hadn't taken long to do the packing and data-inputting. At the start I felt relaxed and on top of things. I was smiling and feeling like me again. Then, as we edged towards the end I became anxious.

We were drip-fed information on how to wind things up and told only partial truths on dates and times and signings, packing up flats and dropping off keys, never really knowing the full story. It was like the end of the year was the first time for everyone – teaching staff, admin, H.R, management - not just me. You would think that after a few years of winding things up at the end of the academic year there would be some systems in place. There didn't appear to be. There was just a panicky chaos where no-one seemed to know what was happening.

Because of the rules around eating and drinking at Ramadan, there was no good bye celebration. There was no end of year buffet with the customary address from the principal. No words of good cheer and congratulations for a job well done, looking to a future of prosperity and continued good work. No final tahdaah! and burst of applause. There was only a ten minute gathering of staff in the theatre to hear the last words from the principal and that was all.

True to chaotic form, not all the teachers were present for the final address. Some of the South Africans and the Jamaican teacher who were travelling on commercial visas were already home. They had flown out to Istanbul, as usual, on their monthly visa turn around, and were told that a further commercial visa would not be issued. The school organised onward flights for them to journey directly home three weeks ahead of the rest of us on full pay. Once again, I experienced just a little passport envy. Flat mates and friends packed up the apartments vacated by the absent colleagues and FedExed their boxes of stuff onwards.

Even on the last day the madness continued like a slapstick comedy. The teachers that had cancelled their civil I.D. glumly hovered round the admin office waiting for their passports to be returned. Marta, the new mum, was in tears. She had been told that her passport had been withheld by the ministry because she had not filed the correct paperwork when she found out she was pregnant earlier in the year. Her flight back to Portugal was that night, in a few hours. The stress of the situation was intense.

A previous year, a Dutch teacher didn't get her passport back from the ministry because, she was told, they had 'lost' it. In a panic, she called the Dutch embassy to see if they could issue an emergency, last minute document so she wouldn't miss her flight which was leaving that night. When she told the person there her name they said that her passport had just been handed in. It had been found outside the Spanish embassy.

Back at the flat I had made an attempt to pack my stuff, which was insisting on spilling out of my suitcase onto the floor like an obnoxious drunk person. I tried to scoop it up and shove it back in, but my stuff now possessed the attributes of a physical living thing and when I stuffed it in one side, some of it came loose and fell out of another.

Finally, I managed to squish everything I had into a suitcase and a backpack for check-in, and have my ancient computer in a carry-on bag. This seemed to work. I would just pay for excess baggage weight at the airport and be done with it, I thought, until I checked in online and realised the cost of carting extra kilograms. I was suddenly embarrassed at the thought of the old rags I had passed for clothes and worn day after day. Why did I want to hang on to these things? Why was it always so difficult for me to dump stuff?

Packing turned into a journey in itself. I could never go ahead and just shed unnecessary layers straight away. First there was the stuffing phase, as described earlier. Then there was the denial phase – casual, relaxed, it'll be fine, but not doing anything about the monster amount of stuff hogging the bedroom floor, until we get to the sensible phase. The day before departure I attain a serenity and a lucid clarity that has a mystical monk-like quality about it. This phase involves emptying the swollen suitcase and systematically holding each item in my hands and asking it if it is coming with me or staying. The things that answer 'coming with' I neatly lay into the suitcase. The things that answer 'staying'; clothes I haven't worn in a year; underwear bought recently, but found annoyingly that the size on the label is nowhere near what it is meant to be; one of many sarongs mum keeps giving me; that skirt that needs mending with the ink stain; a 3D picture of dolphins that swim under water if you look at it one way, and leap together in a family group, if you look at it from another side; an extension lead; a pack of coloured pencils, I leave in a pile on the floor. Some items are unsure how to answer, so I leave them in a separate pile to have a think. At the end of this process I say a fond farewell to the things that have decided to stay. I'm sure they have made the right decision and we go our separate ways as friends.

In the middle of the night I jump out of bed and search through the 'staying' pile to find a favourite t-shirt. *I can't leave you. You're coming with me.*

The last few hours before my flight dragged at an excruciating rate like an injured animal trying to make it to safety.

I hug Helen. Tessa has jumped into a taxi with Dave and they are all gone too quickly. I wave from the side of the road. It's a summer night time, hot at starry. I didn't get to say goodbye to Rupert or Sandra although I know that I shall be seeing them again. Everyone else is on their way. I feel as if I am the only one left in the building. I check around the apartment for the last time musing about my experience in this armpit of the world.

Kuwait is a funny old place. I won't miss it. I will miss some of the people I have met here, but not the country. I will miss the locally grown fresh parsley, spinach and rocket, excellent coffee and dates, but not much else. Kuwaitis have embraced Americanised globalism to the max. They are in love with themed fantasy experiences; shopertainment, edutainment, eatertainment.

I remembered a conversation from our day out at the Hilton.

"Sum up Kuwait in two words," said Tony as he gazed out from the plastic roll-down tent we were occupying on the beach.

"Cultureless void" he mused.

"No-one cares," said Tara after some thought as she dipped an over-priced chip into some red sauce.

"Trying and failing," said Sonia. "Oh no, that's three words."

"Nothing works," I follow up with, soon after.

We all nod sagely.

"Yup, nothing works," repeats Tony quietly. We are all silent for while.

A breeze gently rattles the tent as a white plastic bag skips across the other-wise spotless beach, a reminder that we are somehow inside and protected from the hostile, filthy world beyond the clipped hedges of the five star resort.

Kuwait in two words? Missed opportunity. A missed opportunity of doing things a bit different from the rest of the world with the huge resources from oil revenue.

In a book I read recently by John Hannigan, he quotes sociologist George Lunberg who wrote in 1934 that almost all leisure and recreational pursuits cost money and are thus regarded as "commodities to be purchased rather than experiences to be lived". These ideas resonated with me as a truth of this place. And maybe not just this place, maybe this is the way the world is heading and Kuwait is a synthesized, boiled down, distilled, extreme version of what is happening everywhere.

It is mad here, but Kuwait does not have a monopoly on madness. This is also mad; Jo Cox murdered, shootings in Orlando, Kanye West headlining at Glastonbury. There is madness everywhere. I see it daily in the news splashed across screens and pages; banks bailed out by governments, inhumane agri-business, the last black rhino dies, politicians on a u-turn, pharmaceutical dependency, hair-extensions, commercial fishing, child abuse, burkini ban, Brexit, oppression, injustice, fear, intolerance, hate.

The way I can best sum up Kuwait is if I present the country as a person. Kuwait is a teenage boy, not yet mature and thinking, but fully grown. He would wake up mid afternoon and spend most of the day playing video games, messaging his friends, laughing at the latest 'in' joke, smoking cigarettes and drinking Coca-Cola. When he gets hungry he orders a pizza with extra cheese, chips and a free desert with daddy's platinum credit card. When the food is delivered, he will yell for the maid to answer the door and bring it to him. He doesn't look up from his game when she brings it in. She clears a space on the coffee table and puts it down, carefully picking up empty drink bottles and yesterdays pizza boxes. She does not speak but nods respectfully before leaving the room. He does not say thank you.

I would not be returning for another well paid tour of duty; I had done my time, lived out my sentence. And, after having a sneak peek at the next academic year's calendar, any remaining doubts I had were quickly extinguished. The generous fat holidays that I had enjoyed were slimmed down by a whole week and the school day had been extended; clearly not such a good deal for the same rate of pay. I had ridden the gravy train, oh yes, and now times were a-changing, it was time for me to get off. Here was my stop.

As I closed the door to our apartment for the last time, I caught a glimpse of the purple cup cake sitting, unchanged inside the plastic presentation box with its matching acetate ribbon, smug in its sugary immortality. How long would it be before it disintegrated? I mused, as it surely would, eventually. Could it possibly be eaten before that happened? I shuddered at the thought. Had the cake beneath the icing and sparkling sweets already turned to dust? Was the cup cake an illusion, promising something more beneath the surface? Was the structure of the cup cake was on the brink of caving in on itself - all show and no substance?

That was it. That is what Kuwait is like. Well, it was for me.

Thank you for your attention. I wish you the best.

286